Comeaux Collection

Comeaux Collection

THE FRETTED INSTRUMENTS OF DR. TOMMY COMEAUX

DAVID R. HUSSONG

EDITED BY

SAM BROUSSARD

UNIVERSITY OF LOUISIANA AT LAFAYETTE PRESS

Library of Congress Cataloging-in-Publication Data

Names: Hussong, David R., author.
Title: Comeaux Collection : The Fretted Instruments of Dr. Tommy Comeaux / David R. Hussong.
Description: Lafayette : University of Louisiana at Lafayette Press, 2020.
Identifiers: LCCN 2019058281 | ISBN 9781946160621 (hardcover)
Subjects: LCSH: Comeaux, Tommy, 1952-1997--Musical instrument collections. | Guitar--Pictorial works. | Electric guitar--Pictorial works. | Mandolin--Pictorial works.
Classification: LCC ML419.C646 H87 2020 | DDC 787.8/19763074--dc23
LC record available at https://lccn.loc.gov/2019058281

© 2020 by University of Louisiana at Lafayette Press
All rights reserved
ISBN 13 : 978-1-946160-62-1

Printed in Canada

http://ulpress.org
University of Louisiana at Lafayette Press
P.O. Box 43558
Lafayette, LA 70504-3558

Contents

COMEAUX FAMILY COLLECTION

TOMMY COMEAUX

THE STORIES

Art Strings

They're works of art crafted to create more art. To build community and foster camaraderie. To transcend genres and bridge generations. To make social music and musical statements. To celebrate, commemorate, and inspire.

As you turn these pages, you'll hear their sounds in your head and come across tales that will resonate in your heart. The passion of the builders, the players, and the interconnected friends have all been assembled, first collected by one man whose legacy now radiates outward in uncountable directions.

Most of these instruments' stories began long before they were gathered by Tommy Comeaux and well before they heard the songs in his soul. Today their music spreads farther and wider, and the only place they can still be found together is here, in this singular visual feast of frets, photography, and shared memories.

Musician, historian, writer, and entrepreneur Dave Hussong, photographer Jim France, and designer Megan Barra have lovingly assembled this symphony of strings, and their collaboration has amplified its combined chorus of human achievement. This catalog of so many one-of-a-kind creations and combinations also weaves together thoughts from far-flung folks bound by their love of tradition, innovation, and Tommy.

There's lots to uncover here—from flattops to archtops to resonators to electrics and far beyond. Mostly, though, this volume is a hymn celebrating the power of potential, the joy of exploration, and the value of connection.

There's much more here than meets the eye. Or the ear. And we can thank Tommy for that, and for so much more still to come.

TODD MOUTON

1902
Orville Gibson

This is a stunning example of one of Orville's earliest guitars. Contrasting pieces of abalone and mother-of-pearl surround both the body and the sound hole. This particular guitar is believed to be second in ornate qualities only to one found in the Gibson Museum, which has a butterfly inlaid between the sound hole and the bridge. One of Orville's more exotic designs, it features a cantilevered walnut back, a chambered neck, and friction tuning pegs, all set off a with crescent moon inlaid in the headstock, which could have been the work of a Turkish engraver that Orville had employed at the time. The paper label inside lists the date of manufacture as May 2, 1902.

1918
Gibson Style U Harp

While it could possibly be argued that function does not necessarily follow form where this instrument is concerned, no one can deny its aesthetic beauty. Harp guitars are difficult instruments, but are still in use by high-caliber players such as Steve Howe and the late Michael Hedges. This harp guitar is a thing of beauty regardless of its playability. It would not be possible for Gibson to reproduce one of these to sell at a price point comparable to what they command in the vintage marketplace. Does this make them a good value? If the value is based on aesthetics, they're a steal.

1930
Gibson L-4
Oval

Introduced in 1912, this model has seen as many style changes as any model in Gibson's history. A common derivation had an oval sound hole. Although this orchestral guitar was not necessarily a successful design for big band rhythm, it was favorably put into service by a number of Delta and Appalachian blues artists. By 1935, the company had employed the tried-and-true F-hole design in the L-4 instrument, and by 1949 a florentine cutaway was available.

Gibson

1934
Gibson L-7

Of the four basic derivations of Gibson's tremendously successful L-7, this 16-inch model is an example of the first of the four designs. This model, with the fleur-de-lis headstock, was in production for only a year and a half and discontinued in mid-1934, and must be one of the last of the four derivations.

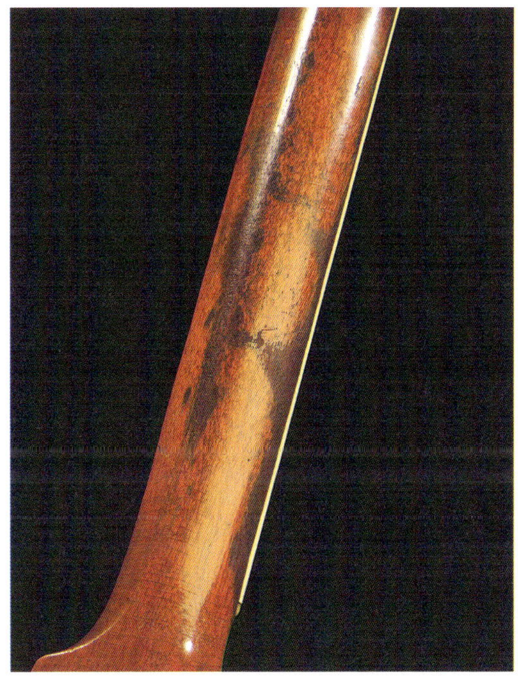

1946
Gibson L-5

This is the standard of the industry as far as orchestral guitars are concerned, starting its run in 1923 with a 16-inch body. It's a pristine example of the modern 17-inch lower bout design implemented in late 1934, and an absolutely functional instrument every bit as attuned to the millennium as it was sixty years ago in the hands of players such as the Nat Cole Trio's Oscar Moore.

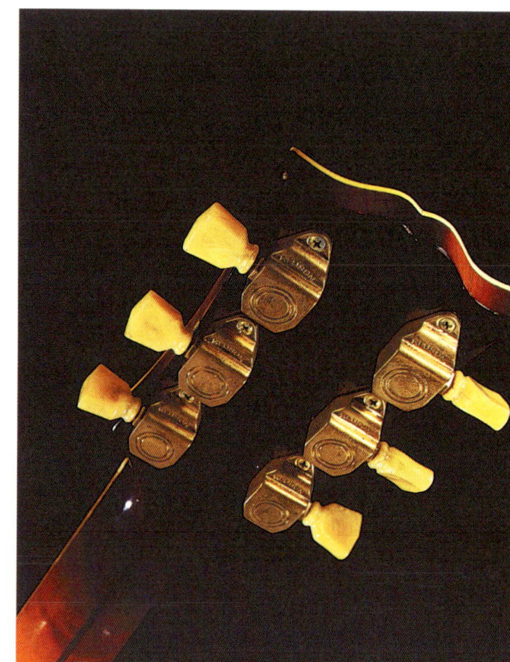

1954
Gibson ES-295

The model designation was derived from its $295 price tag. The ES-295 was essentially a very fancy ES-175 with a real gold leaf finish, an ornate flowered pickguard, and an extended 1952–53 Les Paul Standard trapeze tailpiece. Early in his career with Elvis Presley, Scotty Moore was often pictured with this model. This visually striking guitar was perhaps Gibson's strongest entry into the Rockabilly foray of the mid-1950s. Built from 1952–58, a few of the models made in the last year were stocked with humbucking pickups.

Gibson

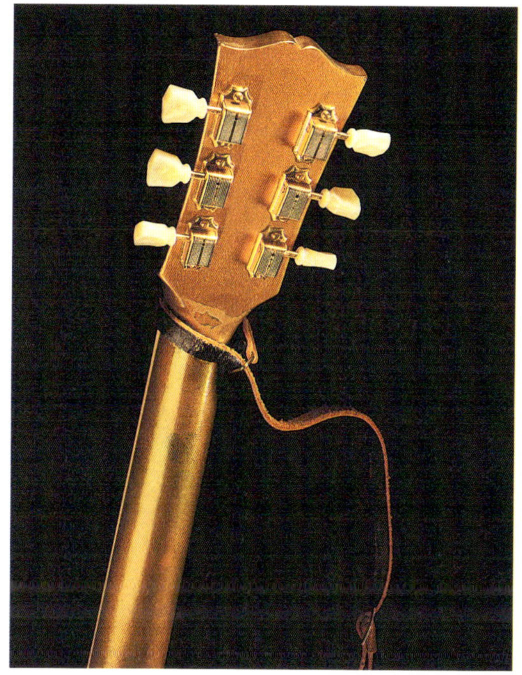

1958
Les Paul Custom

In the eyes of many collectors, this stunning guitar is equal in aesthetic value to the vastly more popular Les Paul Standard of the same time period. Its carved one-piece mahogany body represented a step up in craftsmanship from the Standard, but the lack of a maple cap would make it sonically inferior to its less-expensive little brother. Still, there are legions of players who prefer the warmth that the mahogany construction provides. There were several variations of the 1958–60 models, including the extremely rare two-pickup version, and perhaps the holy grail of Les Paul Customs, the three-knob Mickey Baker model.

Gibson
Les Paul
CUSTOM

1959
Les Paul Standard

The ultimate collectible solid body electric guitar. No two were alike in appearance, this one taking on a greenish hue as the colors faded with the passage of time. This particular guitar, well-traveled between a number of players and collectors, is called Lemondrop.

Gibson
Les Paul
MODEL

1956
Gibson L-5 CES

This stunning, Alnico-equipped variant, regardless of its short production life, still remains one of the most highly collectable electric L-5s. First introduced along with the 1954 Les Paul Custom, the Alnico magnet with its "staple" pole pieces was an upgrade from the P-90 pickup, a redesign for a more balanced low and midrange tonality. After a three-year lifespan, it was overshadowed by the advent of the humbucking pickup in 1957. Scotty Moore and Wes Montgomery were two of this model's proponents.

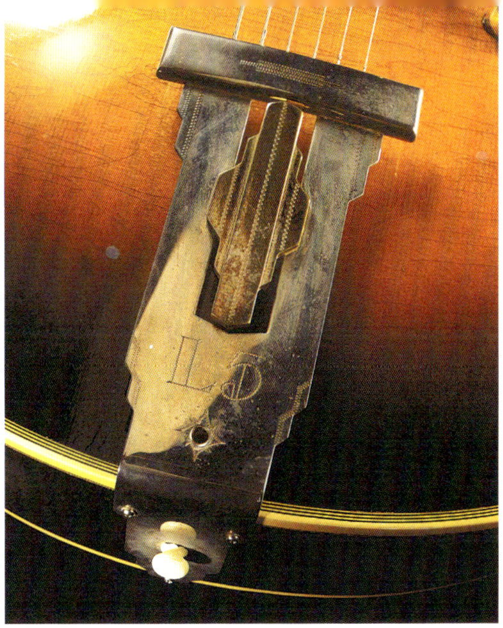

1959
Gibson L-5C

Many guitar historians concur that the pinnacle of Gibson's modern period culminated in 1959. That is certainly true where their electric models are concerned. And you can rest assured that if Gibson designer and endorsee Andy Nelson was alive, he would tell you at great length about the superb archtops Gibson produced at the end of the decade. This beautiful L-5C with its floating pickup would certainly be included in this assessment. In production for thirty-five years at this point, this model perhaps encompasses all the positive aspects of its predecessors. Seventeen inches by this time, full of flame, volume, and balance, it would be difficult to top this example.

1960
Gibson ES-345
Sunburst

One of the "Big Seven" electric collectibles, and favored by blues legends Elvin Bishop and Freddy King, this innovative Gibson model, introduced in 1959, was one of the first instruments designed to capitalize on the stereophonic or dual sound source. It is an incredibly versatile guitar that figures prominently in the geography of popular culture.

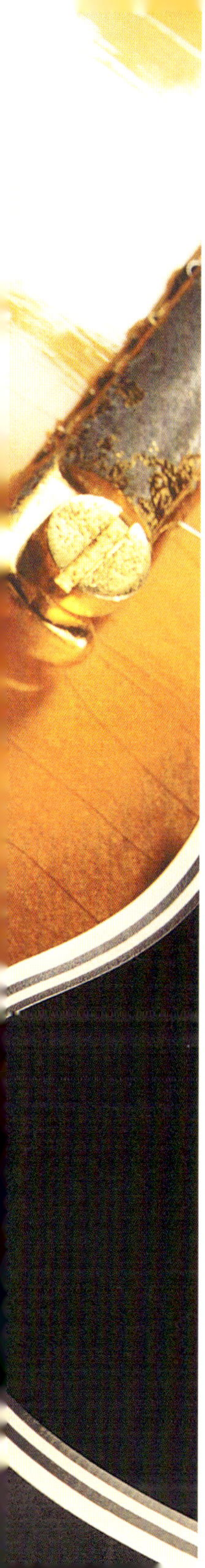

Gibson

1960
Gibson ES-345
DN Blonde

Incorporate all the previous accolades, then consider that this guitar is one of the rarest production models ever constructed in Kalamazoo. The fact that it wasn't built with the ever-popular Bigsby tailpiece makes it even that much more desirable. This beautiful guitar currently resides in very good hands in Toronto.

Coteau: Tommy Comeaux, Michael Doucet, Bessyl Duhon, Kenneth Blevins, Dana Breaux, Gary Newman, and Bruce MacDonald

Tommy Comeaux was an exceptional man, the kind of man you wanted to be associated with. Talented, kind, smart, compassionate, and generous were just some of his many attributes. I'm thankful to have known him as a musical collaborator and a close friend for many years.

We first met when Michael Doucet invited him over to rehearse with Coteau. Tommy was a great guitar player, but the band already had two, so Tommy picked up his mandolin and didn't miss a beat. Soon after, he was one of us, and from that point on we became close friends, playing together in other local bands such as the Clickin' Chickens and Native Sons.

While I had heard of Tommy's collection of instruments and amps, I had never seen it. He didn't want too many people knowing about the treasure he had stored in his home. After all, the Smithsonian had some of his instruments, and collectors from around the world envied the collection. One day I was at his house for a rehearsal, and after the rest of the band left he asked me if I wanted to see his collection. He opened the door to one of the rooms . . . I was blown away! It was full of vintage guitars and basses. Then he opened another room full of amps. Then another full of mandolins, violins, and dobros. I was looking at a museum of very rare and very valuable musical instruments, right there in his home. Then he told me that if I ever wanted to play any (well, almost any) of these to just let him know. I didn't want the responsibility of caring for anything of such high value, so I declined. But not long before Tommy's untimely passing, during a visit I was admiring a 1960s Fender Jazz bass. We were scheduled to have a Coteau reunion at Wolftrap the following weekend, and Tommy told me to take the bass with me for the gig. I reluctantly agreed. After the gig I thanked him for the loan, and right then he told me to just keep the bass as long as I wanted. Well, I couldn't do that. I still had the same concern; I would worry too much about damaging this fine instrument, or something worse. Anyway, he took it back and again told me that I could use it any time. One week later he was killed in a tragic accident.

That's just one of the many stories about Tommy's character and generosity. I still think of him often and miss him dearly. Tommy Comeaux was a talented musician and doctor, but to me his most valuable attribute was that he was an exceptional human being. I'm blessed that he was my friend.

—GARY NEWMAN

1967
Gibson Trini Lopez Red

Part of a series of artist "designed" models implemented initially in 1961 along with the Johnny Smith model, it was obviously Gibson's intent with the release of this guitar to capitalize on Lopez's mid-'60s popularity. Basically a 335 with some aesthetic alterations, such as diamond-shaped sound holes and a non-reverse headstock shape, it has achieved only moderate collectability.

VOLUME

Gibson

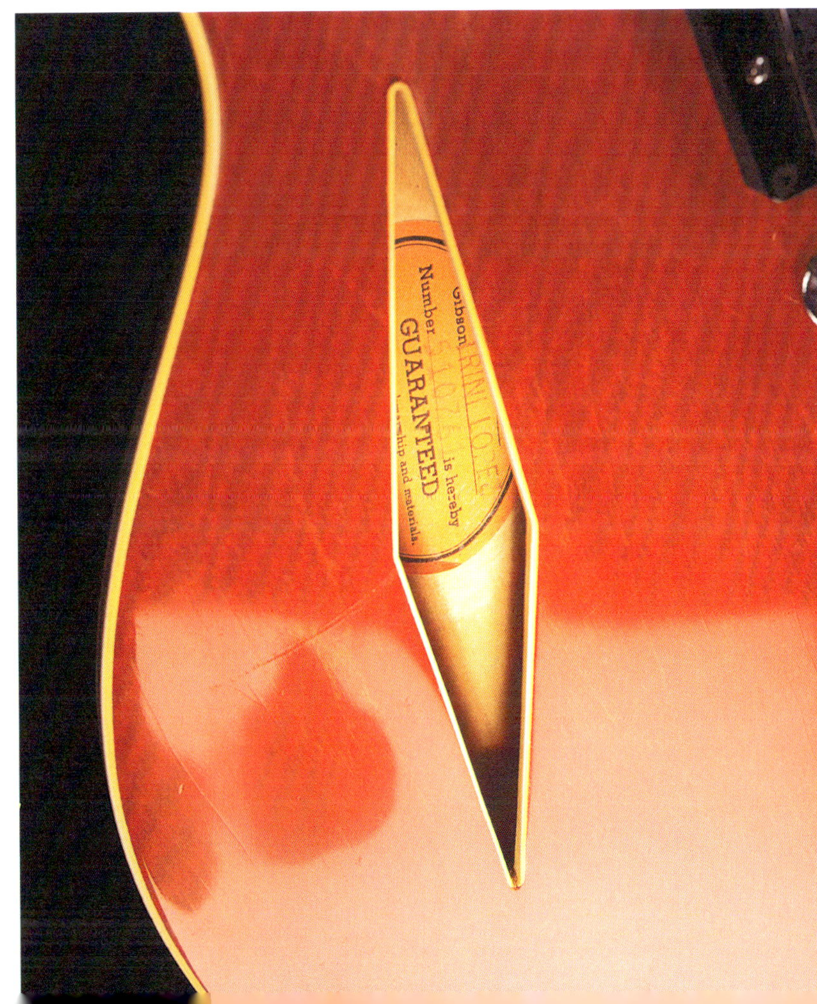
Gibson
Number
is hereby
GUARANTEED

1961
Gibson ES-335
Sunburst

The last full year that the dot inlay fingerboard was available, this ultimate collectable semi-hollow body was characterized by a wide 1 11/16" width to the fingerboard as well as a very flat profile to the contour of the neck. To many players—this writer included—this neck configuration implemented in 1961 along with the PAF pickups constitutes perhaps the ultimate 335.

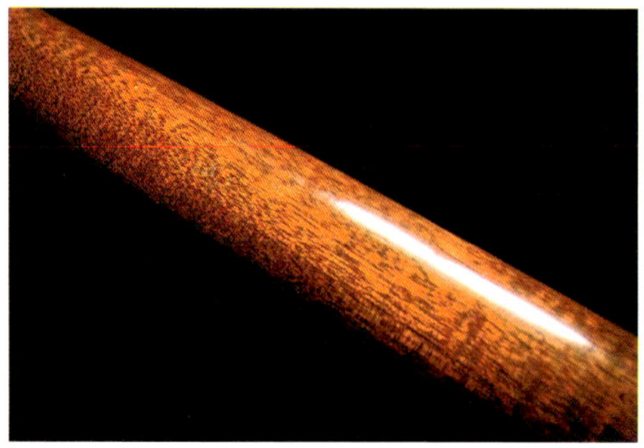

1960
Gibson Les Paul Standard

In 1960, Gibson made some changes to the Les Paul Standard, as found here with the one Tommy located in Montreal, Quebec, in 1994. Most notable of those changes was the slim taper neck and a fix for the cherry sunburst finish that had faded on some of the earlier models. But by 1961, Gibson had discontinued the existing Les Paul design altogether. Then, in 1966, Eric Clapton played his '60 sunburst on John Mayall's landmark release, *Blues Breakers with Eric Clapton.* His quintessential tone and phrasing on that album has inspired generations of guitarists, and the sunburst-era Les Paul Standard has become the most coveted solid body electric guitar of all time.

I've never known anyone who loved to play music more than Tommy Comeaux. He certainly had many talents and interests, but I know that in his heart he was a musician first. He once told me that he couldn't reach his goals as a musician because his responsibilities as a pathologist at the hospital were just too demanding. I had to laugh because any evidence of that was lost with the many bands he'd played in, the sessions he'd played on, and the awards he'd won. How he was able to accomplish so much in both music and medicine still baffles me to this day.

Lots of times when I was off the road, the phone would ring and he'd be on the other end. "Hey man, what are you doing?" was pretty much a call to arms for some of the things we used to enjoy doing together. One was catching up over a cheap and easy dinner at the local cafeteria, where his marathon runner's discipline never went the distance versus their chocolate pie. Or, when he could squeeze it in, we'd meet at one of the theaters for a movie. It didn't necessarily have to be a *great* movie, mind you, but one that would hopefully have a lot of action, or as he'd

Tommy Comeaux and Sonny Landreth, 1984

put it, a "high ninja factor." But our favorite distraction from the world outside was launching into an all-out gear summit at his house. That basically involved us experimenting, checking out different combinations of his amps and guitars along with mine or just blasting for the hell of it. And with his vast, ever-growing collection, I was like a kid in a candy shop. Seriously, it was a guitar player's wonderland over there. He had vintage Martins, original D'Angelicos, Lloyd Loar Gibsons, Chet Atkins Gretsches, a multitude of Fender Strats and Teles from the '50s and '60s, and Les Pauls from '57, '58 and '59, to name a few. But in the midst of all those incredible guitars he had, it was a 1960 Les Paul Standard that I couldn't keep my hands off of, and he really got a big kick out of that. Because of the vintage sunburst finish, I later named it Old Flame.

On the evening of Friday, November 7, 1997, Tommy made the drive out to my place for a change. He'd called earlier to say that he wanted to bring me a copy of the album he'd recently played on, *Highly Seasoned Cajun Music,* by Coteau, a seminal local supergroup that had just reunited after twenty-plus years. There was no mistaking the excitement in his voice. He was really happy with his performance on that project

and for good reason. He had truly come into his own as a player, and as usual, his enthusiasm was contagious. He said that I was always gifting him with my music and now he wanted to repay the favor with the album he was most proud of. He came over after work and gave me the CD and we hung out awhile, talking as he sat on my couch playing one of my guitars. Our get-togethers weren't always just about music—all things life were very much a part of the dialogue. I knew that I could talk to him about anything under the sun and that he would have my back no matter what. But when he left that night and I closed the door behind him, I had no way of knowing that I'd never see him in this life again.

Even in the aftermath of tragedy, his generosity shined. That 1960 Gibson Les Paul? Tommy, being Tommy, left it to me. Though I was moved beyond measure, the mix of emotions was almost unbearable. But there is peace born of friendship that will settle on a soul given time. Whenever I play Old Flame, I think of him and sometimes talk to him as if we were in the midst of one of our gear summits long ago. I can't speak for the other 'bursts that were made that same year, but this one plays like a dream and feels like a conversation with an old friend.

–SONNY LANDRETH

1977
Gibson Les Paul Pro

The Pro made its debut in 1976 and brought with it a return of the P-90 pickup in a production model. This particular example hearkens back to 1968 when the Les Paul Standard rose up from the healthy phoenix of Gibson's golden years. Here we have a rosewood fingerboard, and a pair of P-90s coveted for their "bark." This was the beginning of Gibson's rebirth from the ashes of its mid-'70s quality slump to once again produce a Les Paul of merit.

1987
Gibson Les Paul Standard

Black has always been a popular color; the Standard has always been a popular guitar for the Gibson aficionado. Why not combine the two entities and create a stageworthy instrument that always looks good on film? Sporting full-size humbuckers left over from the Tim Shaw period, a quad of gold "speed" knobs, and a Schaller bridge, this was the Standard in all of its ebony glory.

1992
Gibson Les Paul Custom

The "Black Beauty," and a near mirror image of Tommy's 1958 Les Paul Custom, this is a reissue that predates Gibson's Historic line by a few years. A wonderful return to the Black Beauties of the '50s, we have reissue PAF pickups complete with "Patent Applied For" decals on the bottom of the bobbin plate, black bonnet knobs controlling the volume and tone, and a high-grade ebony fingerboard. The reissue, with its maple top and solid mahogany body, also has jumbo frets, which were a departure from the original Fretless Wonder. A fabulous, newer guitar, whose inclusion completes the collection: a black Les Paul from three different decades showcasing three different pickup configurations.

1992
Gibson Les Paul Classic

Technically named the "1960 Classic," this early '90s Standard in translucent red instantly brings to mind a certain 1958 Standard known affectionately in collector circles as "Sweet Cherry." This Classic has a neck profile closer to the 1960 Standard, which was flatter and wider than pre-'60s models. The nickel-plated covers for the pickups have been removed to expose a dual set of black double coils. Although not particularly "flamey," the see-through red finish makes a statement testifying to its inclusion into a Les Paul collection.

1955
Gibson Les Paul Standard Goldtop

Here we have a Standard that originally came with P-90s and was retrofitted with a nice pair of original Patent Applied For humbucking pickups that included the original mounting rings. The original gold bonnet knobs are in place. In just a few years, this would be the standard electronic layout for all the Goldtops. This Les Paul example personifies the difference between a collector-grade instrument and a player-grade instrument. As a player, I'm drawn to the "old wood" conversion, because it helps me keep some folding money in my pocket. I would also add that this guitar sounded particularly incredible.

1958
Gibson Les Paul Standard Goldtop

Gibson would phase out the Goldtop in 1958 and begin to produce the sunburst Standards that every collector seeks. That being said, this Goldtop is sonically such a standout that it is hard to care what color it is. As if that wasn't enough, it must have spent most of its life under a bed before Tommy acquired it. It's as clean as they come, just spectacular. There's no way to play this guitar without the ghost of Duane Allman calling from beneath your fingers.

1952
Gibson Les Paul Standard Goldtop

The year 1952 was the first year of the Les Paul guitar, an American icon, and therefore a year worth celebrating. The earliest models had distinctive features. The position of the truss rod cover and the Gibson logo itself would reappear on later models. The trapeze tailpiece caused quite a stir. The strings wrapped under the bridge made muting a challenge. It had a glued-on neck, which was 180 degrees from the other solid-body competition of the day, the Fender Telecaster. The rosewood fingerboard, complete with trapezoid inlay and faux mother-of-pearl, joined the single cutaway body shape and gentle, carved archtop. Adding in a pair of single coil P-90s, it all came together to produce one of the greatest achievements in the electric guitar world. Ladies and Gentleman, the Gibson Les Paul!

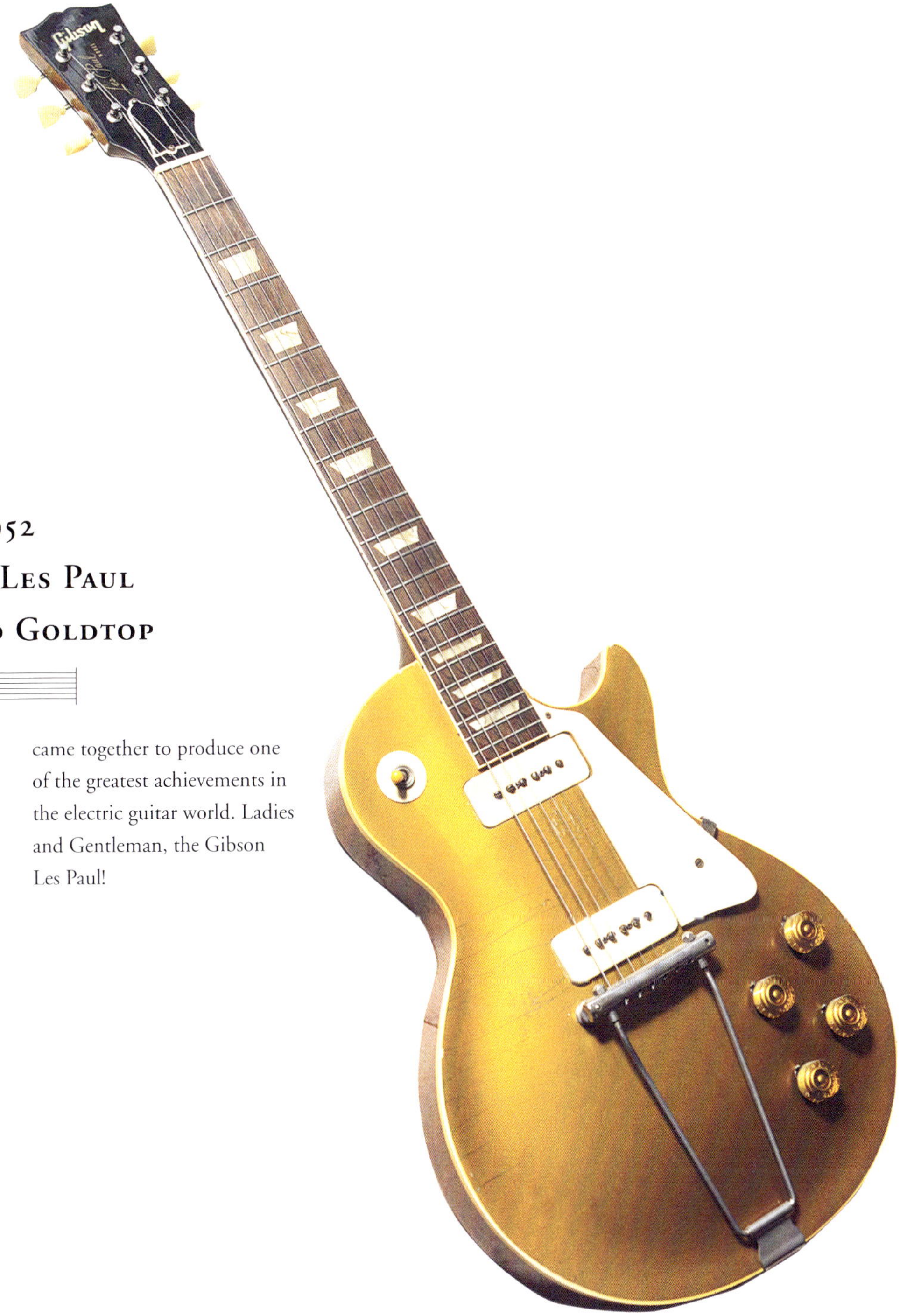

1980
Gibson Kalamazoo Award Sunburst

In 1968, Gibson introduced the magnificent Citation, a 17-inch archtop intended to be a mainstream manufacturer's upper echelon entry into the world of hand-carved instruments. The intention was to retain the benefits of modern manufacturing's more uniform construction techniques, quality control, and other efficiencies. The Kalamazoo Award guitar took the place of the Citation in the late 1970s, and had a moderately successful ten-year run. The one pictured here represents the best of '70s-era lutherie from the company, which was based in Kalamazoo at the time.

1991

Gibson J-200 Black

No, it's not 17 inches! It's actually 16 7/8 inches! Through the years it has enjoyed many incarnations regarding the wood used in the body construction, seeing Brazilian rosewood, Indian rosewood, mahogany, maple, koa etc. One constant has remained: it is "the King of the Jumbo Guitars"—and of course it *was* the choice of a certain Elvis Presley. Whether or not you are attracted to its overwhelming "boom" or its floral decoration—not to mention its deep-waisted body design (the most exaggerated of any guitar's "feminine" shape)—in this case form and function are equally represented. It's a great guitar *and* an automatic stage enhancement. Just ask Emmylou, Little Jimmy, and Bob Zimmerman.

Gibson

1907 Gibson F-2 Mandolin

This three-point mandolin of the post-Orville period has a black finish, the most common on these models. Many of them, including this one, also have an inlaid, flush-mounted pickguard. While the sound is not as open as later F models, these mandolins are certainly sweet and historically important. The body design is Orville's legacy, and while not generally accepted as a great design, all three-point mandolins built later—by any company—are to be considered copies.

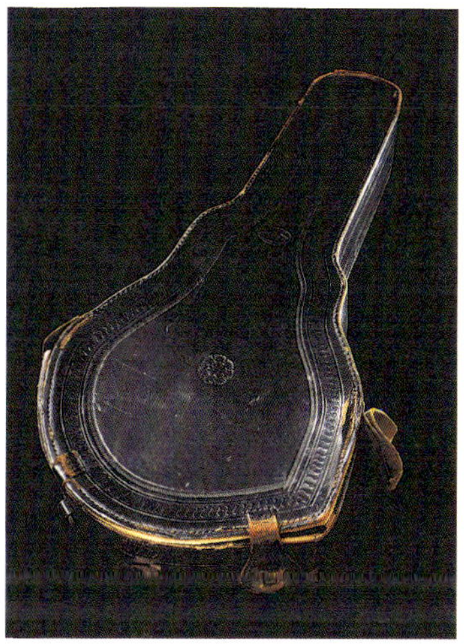

The Gibson

1918
Gibson F-4 Mandolin

This scroll-bodied mandolin has a reddish-sunburst finish, an oval sound hole, and Handel "inlaid" tuners. Top-of-the-line at the time, this model would lay the groundwork for the modern F-style mandolin. Three years later the truss rod would be added, and the F-5 would surpass the top spot with its F-holes and parallel bracing. These mandolins are exceptional values, and while the F-5 models are in the mid-five-digit price (approximately $50,000 at the time of this writing), the F-4s can be had for less than 10 percent of that figure.

PAT. MAR. 30. 09

1915 Gibson K-2 Mandocello

This K-2 mandocello version of an A-4 mandolin has a red sunburst finish and Handel "inlaid" tuners. It is remarkable to find one of these in such excellent condition, because many were converted over the years as the mandolin fell out of vogue. It is primarily classical players and collectors looking to put together a complete mandolin family who seek these instruments.

I met Tommy Comeaux at the annual Labor Day Cajun and Bluegrass Festival in Escoheag, Rhode Island. It was a most unusual festival. Held on an African American-owned dude ranch in rural New England, it had two adjacent stages, which helped keep the music running continuously. There was a dance floor to the side, so dancing was not only allowed but enabled and encouraged. But the most amazing part was the lineup. It was very strong and very diverse. You'd have a traditional bluegrass set, then a great Cajun band, then a singer-songwriter, then a zydeco group, then more bluegrass. If you got tired of one sound, another was coming soon to cleanse your musical palette. Both the performers and the audience seemed to really thrive on the cool mix, and it was all an easygoing symposium for American roots music fans. Tommy played there with BeauSoleil and later with the Basin Brothers, and I played there with Hot Rize and later with my sister Mollie. But over the weekend we all played a little together, onstage and off.

Our accommodations were in a nearby complex of rustic cabins, and there were the usual after-hours hangouts with shared libations and tunes. Food too! I learned from Tommy and the Basin Brothers that Cajuns don't leave Louisiana without special provisions. Where your bluegrasser might buy convenience store chips and dip on the way back to his room, a Cajun would check a whole extra suitcase on the plane to Rhode Island. Contained therein would be a Coleman stove, pots and pans, crawfish, rice, seasonings, and everything else you need for an étouffée. At 1:30 a.m., you'd get a knock on your door and that or a bowl of gumbo handed to you.

Tommy, one of those Cajuns, loved to play every kind of music on his guitars, mandolins, and dobros. It's obvious that he had good taste in instruments. Wherever we met, he'd greet me with his big smile and take me somewhere good to eat, and we'd talk about mandolins and guitars and everything else.

He was such a happy guy—and then suddenly he was gone. I'm lucky to have known him.

—TIM O'BRIEN

1924 GIBSON MANDOLA H-5 LLOYD LOAR

This Loar-period mandola is ultra rare and made of the finest materials, such as two-piece flamed maple back and rims, fern inlay, and a Cremona brown finish. This instrument is just slightly larger than an F-5, and much more rare. This example has the "Virzi-Tone" producer, an internal resonation unit which, at the time, was thought to enhance both tone and overall volume. Virzi was an Italian company that built the Gibson-labeled violins of the period.

The Gibson

M. Campellone Deluxe

A member of the elite modern builder fraternity, Mark Campellone's instruments are of the world-class variety, maintaining the best of the Boston and New York builders of the 1950s and 1960s, while at the same time keeping a focus on the modern approach to solving the mysteries inherent in sound. It suffices to say that Campellone's archtops offer something new under the sun.

M. Campellone
Deluxe

Mark Lacey Apollo

Tommy Comeaux, in the few years that he collected, trusted only a handful of dealers and builders. He had a sixth sense that enabled him to see through the veneer of this industry. No shark lines with Tommy, only reputation and quality. He believed in the future of American-made archtops and in the artisans who maintain the art form. Mark Lacey's magnificent 18-inch blonde Apollo model is a supreme example that conforms to all of Dr. Comeaux's criteria concerning a hand-carved archtop.

Rickenbackers

This venerable company, with roots dating back to California in the 1920s, has always been at least innovative if not blatantly non-conformist, carving out a niche with designs that are unique when compared to the other major American manufacturers. In relation to Martin's flattops, Gibson's archtops, and Fender's solid bodies, Rickenbacker's early cast aluminum instruments and their later semi-hollow bodies fell somewhere between the forefront of innovation and the most adventurous designs from other manufacturers. With lots of points and squared-off angles, there was nothing conventional about their designs. Rickenbacker's flagship instrument has always been their 12-string models, as evidenced here by Tommy's selections.

Rich & Taylor

During his Nashville tenure as head of Gibson's custom shop, Greg Rich established a worldwide reputation for both his inlay work and his meticulous attention to detail. Upon his departure from Gibson in the early '90s, he teamed up with Mark Taylor, Tut Taylor's son, and moved their new business to Murfreesboro, Tennessee, where their work focused on constructing high-quality mandolins and banjos. And yes, they can be every bit as ornate as the Brazilian-bodied dreadnaught in the picture.

Scheerhorn

It's obvious that Tim Scheerhorn's inspiration for this particular instrument came from the Weissenborn line of koa wood Hawaiian instruments. Sheerhorn has been building for several decades, producing instruments endorsed by highly respected players such as Jerry Douglas, Rob Ickes, the late Mike Auldridge, and many others. His production of less than fifty guitars a year ensures his impeccable standards.

I met Tommy on a beautiful sunny day in Telluride, Colorado. I remember taking a call from him and agreeing to meet him down by the stage before the festival started. He told me he was a longtime fan, played mandolin with the band BeauSoleil, and just loved the dobro in general, which was all music to my ears.

Not really knowing who I was headed to meet, I was delighted when he found me first. To meet him thinking he was just a member of a band I liked was barely scratching the surface of how far our friendship would go.

Never again have I met anyone who was so immediately disarming and charming. Something about that "boy growing up proper in the South" was instantly telling on this guy who would become one of my closest friends. We talked a little about how deep his love of music went and how he was only able to revert back to his passion for music when he could get away from his medical practice in Lafayette, Louisiana. Besides being a musician and a collector of great and obscure

instruments, Tommy was a doctor of pathology, having come from a long line of surgeons and doctors. He grew up knowing he would become a doctor, all the while having this other persona of musician. He took it all in stride.

Over the years, my wife Jill and I visited Tommy several times in his home where he housed his collections of rare and beautiful mandolins, Stratocasters, and other great guitars, dobros, and all manner of stringed wonders. His babies. In the backyard he had built a tea house and was eager to extend his Southern hospitality to friends and show them the best time he could in the town he loved.

I was in the beginning week of recording a new project for myself and looking forward to having our mutual friend, Sonny Landreth, on some of the first recordings when I got the call from Sonny that he would have to reschedule because of the tragedy that had taken Tommy's life. That news was incredibly painful, and that whole project has my grief for the loss of Tommy all through it. Life is so fleeting.

I will never forget the love and friendship Tommy gave to me and to everyone who ever knew him. He is forever etched in my memory as someone truly gone too soon, someone who made an indelible mark on how I greet my friends. You never know when the last time you'll see your pals will be, and I cherish the memory of Tommy every time I meet a kind soul. Rest in peace my friend. We will spread the word for you and about you.

—JERRY DOUGLAS
CHRISTMASTIME, 2019

Danelectro Bellzouki

Danelectro, perhaps an ultimate American success story, is shrouded in mystery. The story of their development history, involving both the entertainment conglomerate MCA and the player-repairman-retailer-manufacturer-visionary Dan Armstrong, is too long to recall here. Danelectro enjoyed its greatest success during the period when the company's resident consultant and developer was a young New York session player, Vinnie Bell (thus Bellzouki). Hot on the heels of the success of the electric sitar, Bell jumped from India to Greece with this derivation, available in single and double pickup versions. You can probably still hear it employed on a Saturday night in certain quarters of Detroit.

1990

Ribbecke

At one point, California-based Ribbecke's instruments were finite in number. He closed his shop in 1983 due to allergies to the chemicals in his finishing materials. From that standpoint alone, a certain number of his instruments are attractive to investors, but the instruments themselves, being extremely articulate from both a sonic and visual standpoint, make the luthier's pieces even more desirable. Ribbecke reopened his shop some years ago and is making extremely high-quality instruments.

1981

Guild x-500 Archtop

This stunning blonde was founder Alfred Dronge's answer to Gibson's L-5 CES. While never presenting a real threat to Gibson's archtop line, Hoboken's Guild Guitars offered a high quality alternative to the hand-carved instruments coming from Kalamazoo. Guild's production techniques and quality control have always been held in high regard. During the 1972–82 "lost decade" of diminished quality by some makers, the Guild company never tried to compete with the big numbers cranked out by Gibson, Fender, and Martin, choosing instead to maintain the techniques initiated by Dronge in 1952.

1962
Epiphone Emperor Regent

The lone Epiphone in Tommy's 200-plus instrument collection, it is perhaps the ultimate Epiphone archtop. Granted, it is a Kalamazoo rather than a New York model, having been born after Gibson's 1957 acquisition of Epiphone shortened its independent lifespan and left a number of people out of work. (Many of those people—unwilling to commute, no doubt—were swept up into new employment at Guild.) This 18 1/2" cutaway from 1962 would still be considered by most collectors to be as good as it gets where this model is concerned. It rests comfortably in the hands of an East Coast player/collector.

Epiphone

1990
Larivée
Presentation

This particular instrument demonstrates Wendy Larivée's highly developed inlay artistry. Along with husband Jean's classical approach to building steel-stringed acoustic instruments, this couple has ushered Larivée Guitars into a highly successful Canadian venture. And even with all its ornate qualities, this one is still a tremendous value here in the United States. It is equal in beauty to any instrument, anywhere, for any amount.

Tommy's music room was a rectangular rear addition to his suburban house that contained his B3 organ with its Leslie speaker, his favorite instruments of the day, and his recording console. But

in order to get there, one had to pass his 2,000-plus alphabetically shelved LP collection and his 100-plus acoustic and electric guitars, all resting on their stands in orderly rows. It was like a platoon of silent and at-ease soldiers ready for action. But the coolest thing was the sound that continued when we stopped playing our own instruments, the hundreds of strings from a hundred guitars all sympathetically vibrating around us, how they kept on ringing with octave overtones like a Buddhist gong slowly diminishing in its own time . . .

That reverberating sound was magical! The entire room of silent guitars suddenly awoke and became alive again.

Because they were his, Tommy's guitars were much more than just a collection.

—MICHAEL DOUCET

1982
D'Aquisto Excel Special

This stunning 17-inch-wide guitar is a fine example of D'Aquisto's mature period. It incorporates his design innovations, which include smooth, S-shaped sound holes, ebony tailpiece and pickguard, and a refined, lighter carving. His builds were more lightly constructed than D'Angelico's instruments, making for a more responsive and rich-sounding archtop.

D'Aquisto

1969 D'Aquisto New Yorker Deluxe

D'Aquisto's first fifteen instruments look just like a D'Angelico except for the name on the headstock. He gradually introduced his own ideas, including the smooth choke design and his own methods about carving the guitar. This one still has a metal tailpiece, and is a lovely example of his top-of-the-line New Yorker model.

1990

Foster A5

This beautiful blonde instrument, constructed by Tommy's good friend close by in Louisiana, Jimmy Foster, was one of the luthier's earliest instruments. It shows the influence of Gibson's L-5 CT (thin-bodied L-5s) and their Johnny Smith model, and also maintains an extraordinarily thin radius in the neck profile. It actually feels quite similar to the necks used on Gibsons in the 1961–62 model year.

1990
Foster 7-String

Tommy was a frequent visitor to Jimmy Foster's Covington, Louisiana, shop, north of New Orleans and across Lake Pontchartrain. This is the luthier's first seven-string, and as the story goes, Tommy repeatedly expressed interest in buying it. It's easy to see why; it possesses one of the most beautifully transparent sunburst finishes this author has ever seen. The wide, flat profile of the neck makes it extremely easy to play. Apart from his lutherie, Jimmy Foster was also one of the finest seven-string players in the world.

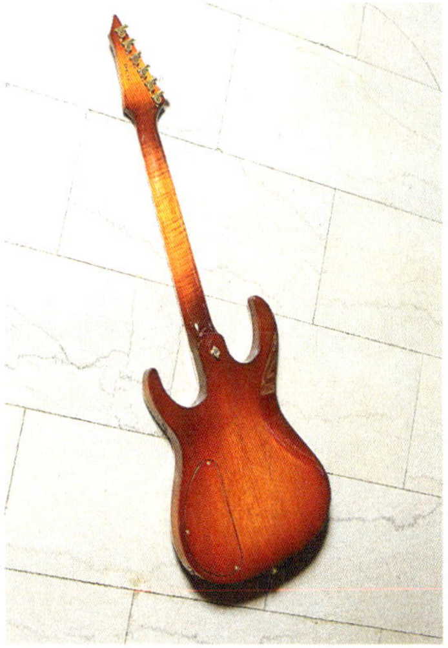

1990
Foster Solid Body

Equally elegant, but not understated by any means, is this pearl-trimmed beauty that incorporates the strongest features of the solid bodies constructed in Fullerton and Kalamazoo. Set neck, contoured body, active electronics, gold-plated parts, and exquisite inlay work make this guitar aesthetically difficult to top.

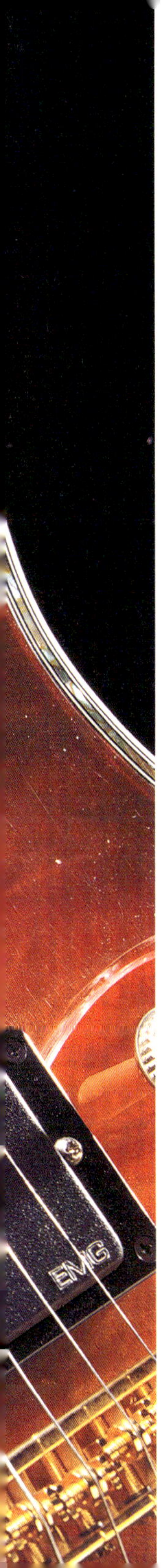

Tommy was my go-to guy when it came to a lot of things. To this day it still pains me not to have my friend to talk to, visit with, to run something by him for his advice.

I first met Tommy at Mulate's restaurant in Breaux Bridge, Louisiana, when BeauSoleil played their Thursday-night gig. People dancing, just having a good time . . . throw in Mulates's gumbo and fried catfish and it was a weekly cosmic event where, over time, a friendship came to light.

And all these years after his untimely death, I can still feel his impact, which I'm sure Tommy would smile about . . . his endowed chair at the university, this book featuring his most prized possessions—his guitars and mandolins!

Not that he didn't enjoy medicine—and not that doctors don't play music—but Tommy was a gigging, touring musician, a complete music guy.

I think I can say that confidently. Remembering the room where he kept the guitar collection, throw in the piano and the home recording studio where he cranked out music for himself and for friends, yep, Tommy was a music guy.

And now his guitars will leap off the page, thanks to this book.

I can see him smiling.

The Rock Guitar God part of Tommy would be happy!

—CHEF PATRICK MOULD

1984
Zeidler Jazz

The first thing I learned about the late John Zeidler—although incorrect—made sense when the incredible accuracy of his work is taken into account. He was not a jeweler as I had been told, but one look at his signature peghead binding will tell you that he could go beyond making a brilliant guitar. His brief apprenticeship with Augustino LoPrinzi was the stepping stone to the current status of his reputation. Equally at home with either a flat-top or archtop design, this koa-bodied Jazz is elegant in its simplicity. It currently resides with a private collector in Hawaii, where they say, "koa rules."

1990

Zeidler

This Excalibur model represents the pinnacle of John Zeidler's acoustic work. The elegant, understated symmetry of the inlay artistry crowning the guitar's beautiful sound creates a combined excellence that would appeal strongly to any collector.

1990

Benedetto Fratillo

Benedetto is perhaps the heir apparent to the throne vacated by the passing of Jimmy D'Aquisto. These examples, although closely related, are as different as night and day acoustically. We couldn't resist photographing their fronts and backs in order to illustrate the dynamic quality of the maple that Robert Benedetto continues to use in the construction of his instruments.

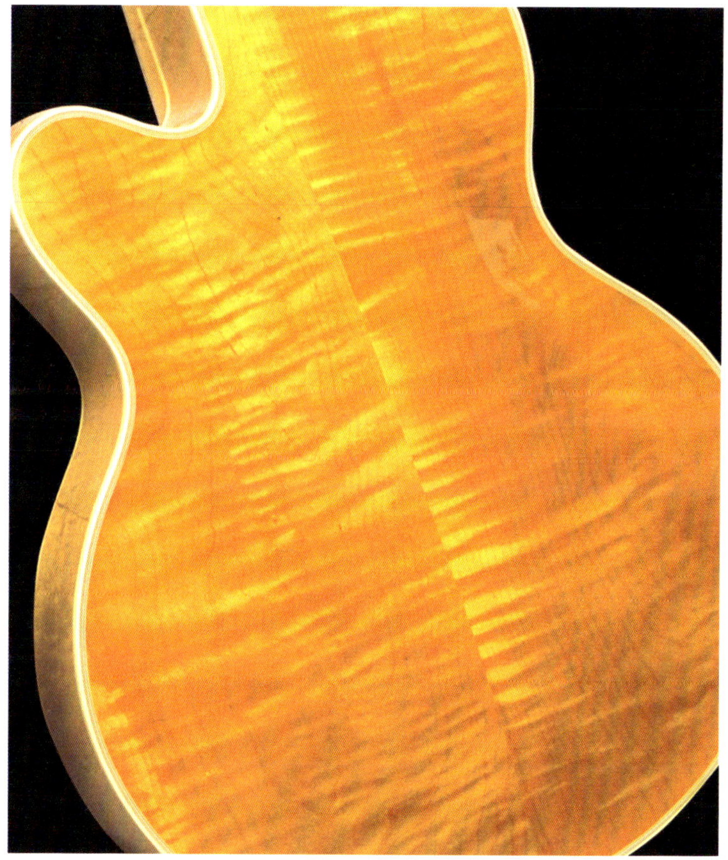

1990
Andersen Metropolitan

It's a rare occasion when form, aesthetic design, and function all come together to create such striking aural and visual results. Seattle-based Steven Andersen's instruments maintain the perfect balance of 1930s art deco design and modern acoustic techniques. While the inlay work is hardly understated, it rests elegantly within the design of the guitar.

ANDERSEN

1990
Andersen
Emerald City

The Emerald City represents Andersen's ultimate art deco design. This instrument looks like it could be part of the Empire State Building, but this showpiece of design sounds as good as it looks. A step up in ornamentation from the Metropolitan, this was the luthier's top model at the time.

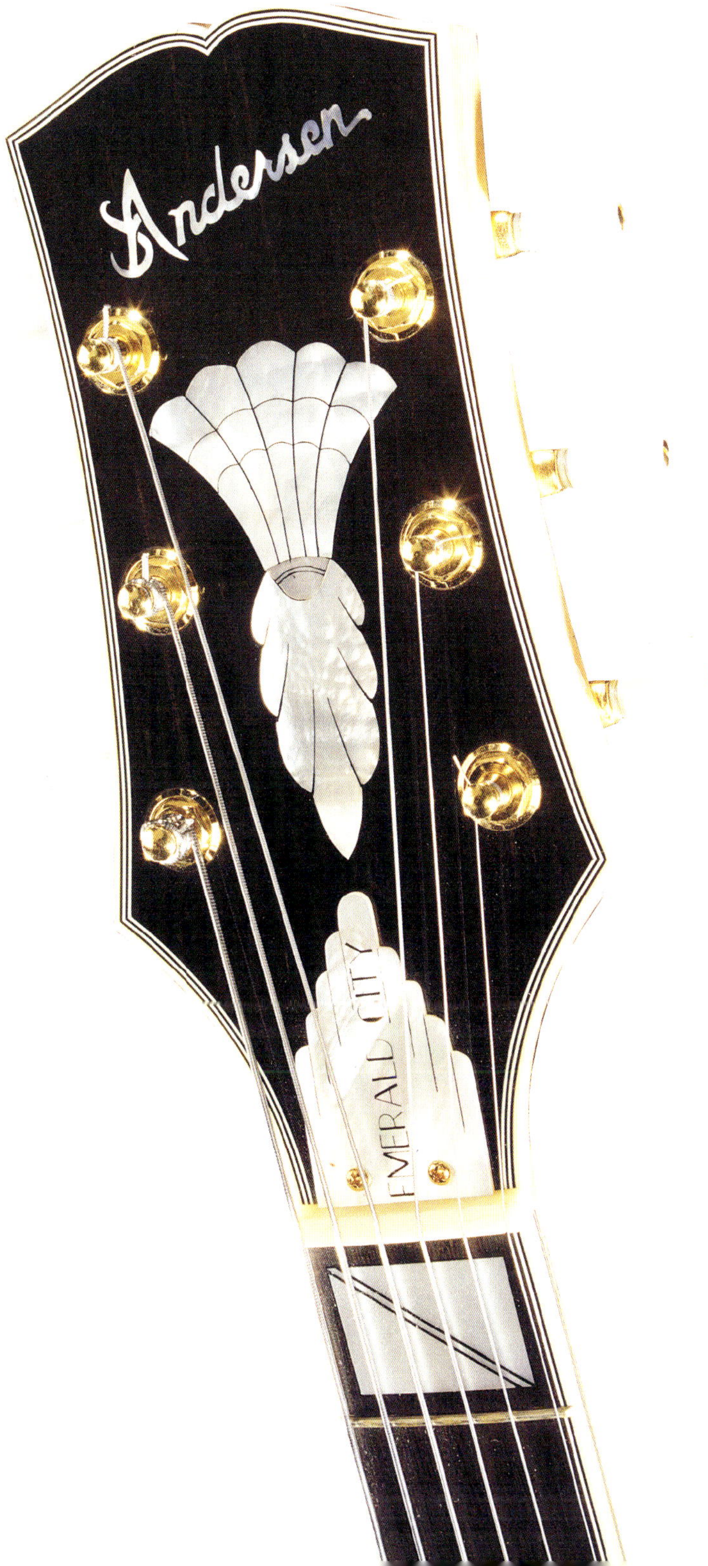
Andersen
EMERALD CITY

D'Angelico Mandolin 150

D'Angelico made about fifty mandolins and divided them into three categories: Plain, Good, and Scroll. Such a naming system suggests a very busy man. This particular Scroll was entered into his ledger as #150 in 1942, regardless of the 1939 date engraved on the tailpiece.

DR. ALFRED E. JOHNS
N.Y.C.
1939

D'Angelico Mandolin 103

This blonde mandolin with the tortoise pickguard, #103, would have been a Plain according to D'Angelico's categorization scheme; the date would be in the neighborhood of 1936–37. We can't have certainty because the luthier's first ledger entry for a mandolin was #125. These are both fine mandolins, but it's the luthier's name that insures their collectibility status.

1947 D'Angelico Excel

This one is documented to be D'Angelico's first cutaway instrument. It has been well-traveled, and despite having endured a number of restoration procedures, this guitar still maintains its original finish. It is an exceptionally good-sounding Excel and is an extremely important instrument in D'Angelico's history. Tommy found this guitar at Mandolin Brothers.

1940 D'Angelico New Yorker

No American builder's instruments are held in higher esteem than those from John D'Angelico. Although there is a difference in sound quality when comparing two like models, there's no argument that the New Yorker defined the art of the archtop in the middle of the twentieth century. D'Angelico was a traditionalist, therefore changes in style and construction appeared seldom through the years. This is a stunning example of a non-cut, blonde New Yorker (his first cutaway instrument was still seven years away). It has astounding presence in both the midrange and bottom-end projection, which is what players from that period needed to cut through the brass section. This instrument currently resides in Dallas, Texas.

D'Angelico
NEW
YORKER

1940 D'Angelico Style A

Both Style A and Style B instruments were entered into the ledgers in 1936. Both styles being 17-inch instruments and having parallel bracing, they were also very similar in construction, with the Style A having slightly less ornamentation. Most Style As, including this one, maintained a dot-inlaid fingerboard. This one has been professionally refinished and the tuners were replaced, most likely in the 1950s. It has a sonic quality similar to a block-inlay 16-inch Gibson L-5, and perhaps favors the sound of Eddie Lang's instrument.

1940 D'Angelico Style B

Of the three D'Angelico orchestral models (non-cutaway) that Tommy had in his collection, this Style B is acoustically hands down the winner. You can play a Freddie Green single-note passage (a rarity) and the guitar maintains equal projection for each note within the line. It is a magnificent instrument that exemplifies D'Angelico's sense of elegant understatement and Old World appointments.

1964 Martin Brazilian 0021

Brazilian rosewood back and sides, Sitka spruce top, and the “tongue depressor” bridge come together in the smaller but very potent OO size from Martin. This particular nylon-string brother of the OO-28 steel-string is absolute magic. What I would consider a sleeper from an investment/collector point of view—all that goes out the window with a few simple strums. If you really want to find your acoustic soul, I suggest hunting one of these down and seeing what your heart and hands can produce. So easy to play . . . and so hard to stop.

Don't Hesitate

I knew Tommy in the eighth grade, but not well, nor did I hang around him a lot as an adult—I just wasn't here in Louisiana; I was living it up in a place with real winters. I arrived back home around '96 without a decent acoustic guitar, one that a microphone would love. One night outside of Randol's restaurant, Tommy told me he had a nice Martin D-35 for me until I could supply myself. Walking into his house, I saw through an open door what appeared to be many upright guitars surrounded by walls of mirrors that multiplied their number. No mirrors of course; it was a big room, and guitars filled it like a phalanx of colorful little Roman soldiers.

Since Tommy was a good guy—a *really* good guy—I know now that those things were another way for him to connect with people. That sounds too easy, but wait. Later that night, after drowning in his carved wooden dreams—I remember something with a serial number of 0002—we went into his recording studio and he called up a fully-arranged song that he had written. I don't remember the title, but the content was about that connectivity. He gently sang that he badly wanted everyone to feel it, because it's just true. It was so *him*. I asked around if anyone else remembered that recording, but after the dust had settled, after all the confusion, it was never found. Three and a half minutes of Tommy's soul, sung on pitch. It's all just part of the ache.

Here's a thing you should know: regarding Doctor Comeaux, he told me and lots of other folks, "If you need help in the middle of the night, call me. Don't hesitate." That's how I remember it, word for word.

Some of my old friends call that "in-service."

And we all watched Tommy juggle his overwhelmingly full life of medicine, music, working out, and collecting. I mean, come on . . . so I asked.

"Tommy, what about a . . . social life? You know, outside of this. Got one?"

He didn't live like a monk but he could see the monastery from where he was, so he answered, "I want three things in life. I only have time for two."

A year passed, and I asked him a more general question.

"Tommy, how do you do all this? I mean, come on . . ."

He answered, very simply and without irony, "I'll sleep when I die."

Here's another thing you should know: that man went to the chapel in the hospital across from where he worked every day and got down on his knees and prayed for the rest of us. He *prayed* for us, you and me, *every day*.

There you go, and evidently that's how you do it: wake up, make the world a better place, go to bed tired. I'll only add that his playing seemed transformed to me in 1997. The last time I heard him, it seemed that all his natural soulfulness and diligent practice was coming together that night at Grant Street Dancehall, composed-but-not-really stuff coming out of that pretty blonde 345—perfectly integrated, just like all his Tommy parts. He was playing so well right before he left.

—SAM BROUSSARD

1990
Schoenberg Martin Custom

Brazilian. You'll hear that word a lot in the finer acoustic guitar collections. Why exactly, does Brazilian sound better? I don't really know. I know only that it does, and so does Eric Schoenberg, who collaborated with Martin over an eight-year period. Together they produced an extraordinary triple-O, as seen here. From the fingerboard to the headstock, the matching of the lines in the grain show the attention to detail that Schoenberg is known for. A gorgeous abalone rosette completes an understated masterpiece. With this guitar, Dr. Comeaux owned one of the finest triple-Os I've ever heard from any era.

1992
Collings Clarence White

When asked if there is a standout in the Comeaux collection, I respond with "many." That being said, this Collings CW is without any reservation the most incredible dreadnaught I have ever played. With Bill Collings's dedication to re-creating the large sound hole 1935 D-28 that Clarence White played, complete with Brazilian back and sides and Adirondack top and braces, the gold standard was created, in my opinion, for all D-size guitars to come. Adhering to pre-war Martin specs certainly helps, but Collings added something besides the enlarged sound hole to this one that I've never found duplicated. It truly is like holding a 9-foot Steinway in your lap.

1993
Collings D2-H Brazilian/Adi

Collings guitars are well represented in Tommy's collection, and for good reason. The craftsmanship and attention to detail is second to none. He had twelve of the Austin luthier's guitars, and every one is sonically without peer in a collection of over 200 instruments. Collings knows his Brazilian and Adirondack tonewoods, and the way he blended the two is absolute heaven for the player.

1940
D'Angelico Style B

To hold something in your hands that was also held by the master builder of the archtop, John D'Angelico . . . well, "giddy" just isn't strong enough. Although his work is featured earlier in the book, I cannot say enough about the power of this particular guitar. Whether single notes (especially the top strings) or chordal work, this guitar personifies all that is D'Angelico. From across the room, the projection of this Style B is sure to command your attention. A fantastic instrument.

1980s
Guild B-50 Acoustic Bass

The B-50 is the alternative to lugging a big doghouse bass around. The quality of the this Westerly, Rhode Island, instrument is without peer, and being able to plug it in expands the usefulness of both itself and its owner. There weren't but a few selections for the acoustic bass in the 1980s, and the Guild B-50 was at the top of the menu. The B-50 features a split saddle bridge, a very easy neck, and it sat on your lap . . . what else could you ask for?

1970
Martin Style 21

This small-body instrument represents Martin's transition to Indian rosewood in 1970. The next step up from the Style 18, the 21 offers Indian rosewood sides and back with a Sitka spruce top. The slotted headstock remains unchanged from previous years. Not quite as fancy as the Style 28, it made for an excellent buy for the singer/songwriter with a passion for a rosewood guitar's tone. The internal 1/4-inch bracing helps produce a big sound from such a small guitar.

1981
Martin
HD-28

The HD-28 came on the scene in 1976. It differed from the previous D-28 in that it now had scalloped internal bracing along with Herringbone trim, a redesign with the magic to transport the player back to the Herringbones of the pre-war/war-time era. It was an instant success for Martin, and would pave the way for the return to other cosmetic and structural designs of the original D-28. The HD-28 remains a favorite in bluegrass circles for that big, airy bass tone and lively top end.

1984
Lowden
O-25

Richard Thompson may be the most well-known advocate of Lowden guitars. They adapt well to different tunings, and the voice is recognizable from across the room. This Jumbo O-size features a cedar top and rosewood sides, and, the tuners excepted, virtually every part of this guitar is created from wood. It also features maple binding as opposed to plastic, and a stunning handcrafted rosette. The O-25 is a joy to play and could possibly infuse your playing with a measure of Thompson's brilliance and fire. The Lowden has been built in different parts of the world; this one was born in the small shop of S Yairi builders in Nagoya, Japan.

1990
Henderson
D-28

Now that he's retired from the post office, Wayne Henderson no longer has to fit a 9-to-5 job into his playing and building time. The award-winning fingerpicker has been building guitars highly prized in the bluegrass circles that spend time looking for the perfect D tone. Big, bold, balanced are words that are commonly used to describe the Henderson. His instruments are easy to spot with the their signature bridge pin placement, but the final words are: to play one is to want one. The waiting list could be long, so you may have plenty of woodshed time to make yourself worthy before your trip to Rugby, Virginia.

1990
Dexter Johnson
12-String

Dexter Johnson is a legend, the man that other luthiers have turned to when they want to get the most outlandish in their search for Brazilian rosewood. This magnificent 12-string is an example of some beyond-the-beyond Brazilian exotica. From brilliant orange to black and every color tone between, it's hard to take your eyes from the back of this guitar.

1965
Gretsch Country Gentleman

Before February 9, 1964, the Country Gentleman sat in relative obscurity near the top of the Gretsch lineup. All of that changed when the Beatles made their historic first appearance on the Ed Sullivan show. From that point on (and almost overnight), the Country Gent became THE guitar to own. The waiting list grew to over a year, and by 1967 it seemed that every English band had a Gretsch Country Gentleman in tow. Double string mutes, the iconic Bigsby, a Supertron pickup for the neck, and a Filtertron pickup in the bridge—it all came together to produce the highly distinctive sound that is unique to the Gretsch guitar.

1966
Gretsch 6119 Tennessean

Chet Atkins also used the 6119, first with the single pickup model and later in the configuration shown here in Tommy's collection. George Harrison was another prominent user. The 6119 featured the HiLotron pickups, a Bigsby, a single cutaway, and Atkins's signature on the pickguard. Like other Gretsch models made after 1959, it features a zero fret and faux F-holes—these are actually decals!

1968
Gretsch 6120 Nashville

Probably the most iconic of the Gretsch lineup, the 6120 found its way into popular music in the mid-'50s as a single cutaway hollow body with true F-holes and DeArmond Single Coil "Dyna-Sonic" pickups. It went through several changes over the next ten years and became the guitar now known as the Nashville model. The late '60s era Nashvilles sported the orange finish, decal F-holes, thumbprint fingerboard inlay, a zero fret, Filtertrons, the Gretsch Bigsby, and last but not least, the double cutaway body with the removable cushion pad on the back for easy access to the electronics inside. Wanna hear one? Grab Chet Atkins's album *Teen Scene!*

1940s
Gretsch Synchromatic 160 Cat's Eye

Introduced in 1939, the Synchromatic Archtop achieved considerable success from its beginning as a go-to guitar for orchestra players looking for something different and a little more affordable than the Gibson archtops. This particular guitar displays rare tortoiseshell binding, "forward slash" fingerboard inlays, and an abundant amount of flame on the back and sides under a blonde finish. All of that and the cat's eye sound hole make for a stunning visual display of art deco wonderfulness. And it sounds pretty darn good as well!

1957
Gretsch White Falcon

Of all the colors offered in the Gretsch line, the Falcon with its gleaming white finish was the flagship of the Brooklyn-based builder. Among all the Falcons that have flown through the years, none captured the imagination of collectors like the original issue from the 1956–57 period. Jeweled knobs, engraved inlays, gold sparkle binding, Cadillac tailpiece, and in this instance, a Lucite pickguard supported by white felt spacers mounted underneath . . . it all makes this rare bird of prey a step above all the others at the top of the line.

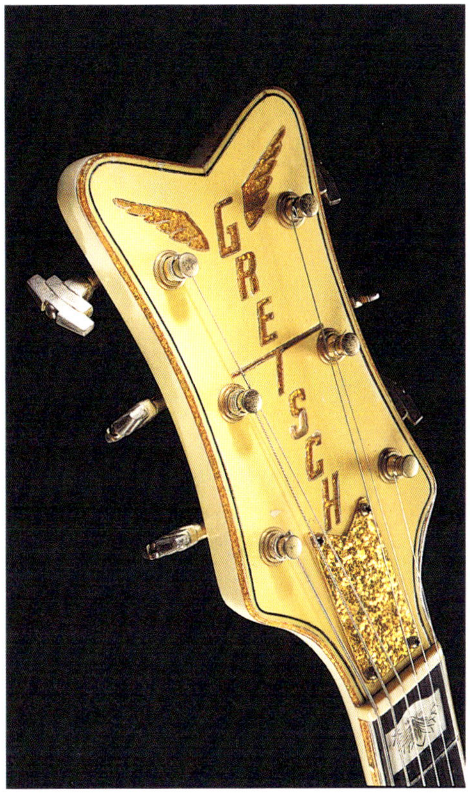
GRETSCH

GRETSCH

1958
Fender Stratocaster

What can be said that hasn't already been said about this model? Tommy loved Stratocasters, and this is an especially clean example of an early three-toned maple neck. The year 1958 was a transitional year for the red being added to the yellow and black finish as well as the departure from a V-shaped neck profile to a more rounded contour. Many 1958 Strats are characterized by a very white-ish appearance to the maple in the necks. If you search long and hard, you might find one of the very first slab rosewood-necked Strats from the latter part of this model year.

1972 Fender Telecaster

Modified with a mini-humbucker in the neck position and a Parsons-White B-bender, this Telecaster is definitely loaded to be a true workhorse. Covering twang country all the way to deep jazz refer yourself to Ted Greene or Sam Brown—it's all been done by the deceptively simple Telecaster, which shows no sign of fading away. Many players will drop in a humbucker for a fatter treble, but the well-known Tele snap provided by a maple neck and that iconic single coil bridge pickup holds the ultimate truth in the 1950 design.

1966 Fender Telecaster

Steve Cropper, Mike Bloomfield, Jimmy Page . . . a white Telecaster sporting a rosewood fretboard was often seen in the hands of these Tele masters. The 7.25 radius feels different on the mid '60s Teles, and at higher volumes, wood and radius produce a tone that can't be found in the maple fretboards. But this particular 1966 nailed the Buck Owens/Don Rich tone in spite of that rosewood. This is a favorite among so many, and a true American classic.

1990 Simpson Telecaster

Tommy was a fan of the B-bender. It shows up on three of the Teles displayed here. While not much is known about this particular builder, the guitar itself plays like a dream and is a departure from the others utilizing the Hipshot Bender approach. The fit and finish and its reverse Tuxedo decor make it a standout. You don't have to be a world-famous builder to be included in the Comeaux collection, just build a world-class guitar!

1959 Fender Telecaster

Many would shy away from a refinished instrument. Not Tommy. This impeccably done sonic blue '59 is a delight to play and gaze upon. Historically, this would be one of the last maple neck Telecasters before the switch to the slab rosewood board in mid-1959. All other aspects of this Sonic Blue specimen were original to issue.

1978 Fender Telecaster

A Gene Parsons-White B Bender is professionally installed in this otherwise bone stock '78 Telecaster. Even with the Bender's mechanics and the substantial routing required to accommodate one, this guitar remained quite heavy, in keeping with a lot of late '70s Telecasters.

1961 Fender Stratocaster

A 1961 Charcoal Frost Metallic Stratocaster would be extremely rare, even if that color was a refinish, especially since that color was not available till 1965! If you're going to collect custom color Stratocasters, you take what you find and refine the collection as you go. With everything else on this slab board being original to issue, it attains lead-dog status of the custom color Strat Pack as we travel through Dr. Comeaux's collection.

1965 Fender Stratocaster

This original 1965 Lake Placid Blue may look familiar. It was acquired from Eric Johnson and was seen on tours and covers of well-known guitar magazines. There is much more to this one than just a splendid, well-cared-for Lake Placid Blue finish. It is one of the most resonant veneer boards I've ever played, and it has a fantastic set of original pickups. A very clean specimen, seeing that custom color instruments seem to get more finish-fragile over time.

1990 Eric Clapton Signature Stratocaster

Mr. Clapton's Stratocaster was the second signature guitar to emerge from the hallowed halls of Fender USA in 1988. It has remained a stalwart in their signature line with only a few changes to the electronics over the years. This mint 1990 model is displayed in Pewter Grey Metallic. With active electronics and their extra 25db boost, it could approach the output of a dual coil humbucker while offering a wide palette of tonal colors from the Lace Sensor pickups seen here. The tremolo bridge block has been removed and the tremolo itself has been set up to use as pitch-down only.

1989 Strat Plus

Here's an interesting guitar: a Strat Plus from 1989 dressed in Midnight Wine metallic finish, stocked with a set of Lace Sensors, a roller nut, and a Roland Hexaphonic pickup for accessing synth sounds from a Roland processor or other midi sound source. It is a beautiful guitar ready for both traditional Strat moves and modern explorations into the more produced sounds of the recording studio.

1990 Eric Clapton Signature Stratocaster

Dubbed the 7-UP model, this color was actually Candy Apple Green. Identical to the collection's Pewter Grey Clapton model in every aspect with the addition of a few other specs that players find desirable, namely the soft V-neck profile, the 9.5-inch radius fingerboard, and the satin finish of the neck. It continues to be a modern classic and a Fender best seller.

1994 40th Anniversary Fender Stratocaster

Number 116 of 1,954 guitars built to commemorate the fortieth anniversary of the Stratocaster, which began its production life in 1954. Fender developed an instant collectible with this model because of the attention to detail. The guitar came with two cases, one of which was the coveted "poodle case" reminiscent of the earliest Fender Strat cases. A larger profile neck with body contours from the Strat's earliest days made this a true modern treasure.

1961 Fender Stratocaster Fiesta Red

Perfection? Maybe. For many, this would be the *crème de la crème* of the '60s-era Stratocaster. With its original Fiesta Red finish to the slab Brazilian rosewood fingerboard and distinctive headstock curve, this pre-CBS model is striking, and the pinnacle for some Stratocaster collectors. If the maple neck '50s version evokes Hank Marvin, then the '60s version definitely evokes the late Gary Moore.

1965 Fender Stratocaster Dakota Red

A very late 1965 Stratocaster, and what we would call a transitional model. It retains the small headstock, but the serial number beginning with 100xxx and the heraldic F on the back plate let us know this is indeed an early CBS Stratocaster. Its most striking attribute is the beautiful Dakota Red finish, which is rare in any era.

1966 Fender Stratocaster Candy Apple Red

The year 1966 ushered in several changes after the CBS acquisition, the larger headstock most noticeably. Upon closer inspection, the headstock decal now revealed five patent numbers. The pickguard was no longer celluloid, and beneath it were other changes such as the color of wiring used, and the neck date stamp now had an identification code attached to it. But standing above and beyond all of these changes is the beautiful Candy Apple Red finish.

1964 Fender Stratocaster Burgundy Mist

For a slight upcharge of 5 percent, Fender solid bodies were available in custom colors borrowed from the automotive industry. The Dupont Duco color chart provided choices for what would become some of the most-sought after Stratocasters, and this particular Burgundy Mist finish is one of the rarest. Although this Strat's finish is not original to the guitar, it was impeccably done and is a visual stand-out in the Comeaux collection.

1966 Fender Stratocaster Sunburst

This 1966 sunburst Stratocaster features a larger headstock, the primary transitional feature that announced the acquisition of Fender by the Columbia Broadcasting System. Showing some wear on the upper body contour, this one saw enough playing time to leave a mark. A sure sign of a well-loved guitar.

1962 Fender Stratocaster Sunburst

Players and collectors alike share an affinity for the slab rosewood fingerboard, which made its debut in 1959 and lasted until mid-1962. The company then changed to a thinner, veneer board. This particular '62 has seen a refinish and an extra string tree added. For the purist, the collectable aspect is gone. For the player, not so much. This guitar is one to keep and play, and is one of the collection's standouts for the tone of its middle/rear pickup selection.

1965 Fender Stratocaster Candy Apple Red

As mentioned, 1965 was a transitional year for Fender, and the Stratocasters saw their share of design changes. This is an early 1965 example with pearl dot position markers, perhaps a more stylish upgrade from the clay dot markers of 1964. Celluloid pickguards with their mint-greenish hue were now replaced with a white ABS plastic pickguard. This lovely lady is dressed in perhaps the most popular custom color finish of 1965, the spectacular Candy Apple Red.

1958 Fender Stratocaster Fiesta Red

Images of Hank Marvin and the Shadows ripping through "Apache" instantly come to mind when viewing this 1958 Stratocaster. The Fiesta Red color became so iconic that the sunburst models imported to England during the Shadows' heyday were often resprayed in Fiesta Red in an effort to meet the demand for a Strat like Marvin's. While this one does not have gold-plated parts, it does have Eric Johnson's signature on the back of the headstock!

1961 Fender Stratocaster Daphne Blue

Imagine the dilemma of heading out to the gig and the bandleader has requested that you bring a Stratocaster, preferably something in Daphne or Sonic Blue. Since you're imagining, why not this beautiful slab board Daphne Blue? Because they were rare, that's why not, and thus its inclusion here. This is an extremely clean representative of the Leo Fender and Dupont color collaboration, and a very hard color to find in any condition.

1990s Fender Stratocaster Reissue

Finished in what appears to be Inca Silver, this guitar represents Fender's ability to go back into the archives and create a modern vintage masterpiece. The '90s slab board lacks some of the detail aesthetics of the early '60s but still brings it all home with outstanding electronics and playability. Another thirty years down the road and this may be the most desirable Strat out there.

1997 Fender Stratocaster Shoreline Gold

As mentioned previously, the object of collecting custom-color Fenders is to acquire what is available and refine that collection as you go. A Shoreline Gold Stratocaster is very hard to find from any era, so this one will do nicely until something "a little more vintage" comes along. Particularly noteworthy here is the size of the flake in this finish. It invokes the spirit of the early Dick Dale guitars but in a different color. It is an absolute beauty, and it shows Fender's dedication to bringing back the good stuff.

1963 Fender Stratocaster Sonic Blue

Rounding out the Comeaux Stratocasters, this veneer board Strat is a true beauty with just the slightest bit of wear showing on the upper contour where the arm would rest. The easiest way to determine the general time frame of this guitar's production would be the headstock decal, the curved veneer fingerboard, and the pickguard screw placement, most noticeably the screw by the middle pickup on the upper side of the pickguard.

I first met Tommy when I was on tour through Louisiana in the 1980s. We visited a number of times after that over the next few years.

He was always so friendly and passionate about music; his sweet spirit I will always remember.

As I look back, I realize now how humble he was. He never mentioned to me about all his accolades, about being a doctor who administered to the needs of so many, or his tireless work for the community. And I never fully realized the extent of his instrument collection.

His preferred "instrument of choice" was being kind to others and sharing happiness . . . the simple and beautiful treasures in life. Could one make a more magnificent choice?

—ERIC JOHNSON

1990
Collings Archtop
#30

If you are going to start a guitar company, location may not be everything, but blooming out from a new music capital sure couldn't hurt. This Austin-based luthier incorporates in his acoustic instruments the most formidable qualities that Nazareth, Pennsylvania, had to offer prior to 1970. But many collectors and afficianados feel that Bill Collings took up where Martin left off.

Collings

1990
Collings Archtop
#3-90

These are extremely rare to begin with, but as a few fortunate collectors can attest, they are more than worth the wait. Incorporating influences from Lloyd Loar to Jimmy D'Aquisto, Collings 17- and 18-inch carved-top guitars have been literally and figuratively molded to the aural and visual interests of the prospective buyer.

1990 Collings Archtop Sunburst

This particular instrument embodies many of the aspects of the L-5s made by Gibson from approximately 1924–32. Sonically, it brings to mind the sounds of Eddy Lang and Eddie Durham.

1930 National Style 4

The quest for a louder acoustic guitar culminated in 1927 with National's "tricone" guitars, which featured three spun aluminum cones functioning as loudspeakers. This is National's original entry into the guitar market, and the three-resonator model that preceded the single-cone Triolian. These metal-body resonator guitars were offered with either a round "Spanish" neck or a square neck for Hawaiian style. They stood out in a crowd with their gleaming German silver (a nickel alloy) engraved with floral motifs. Style 4, the fanciest, wore chrysanthemums and sold for a list price of $195. Their high volume made resonators an immediate success, but they were just as quickly overshadowed by the early amplified guitars of the mid-1930s.

1933 National Triolian

Despite having "tri" in its name, National's Triolian has only one resonator cone. After introducing metal guitars with three resonator cones to the world in 1927, National discovered that the $125 price on the cheapest model was beyond the reach of many players, so they quickly developed a one-cone model. The oddly-named Triolian debuted in 1928 with a wood body, but by the end of 1929 it was steel. With an affordable price tag of $45 and a sound that was considerably louder than a standard guitar, the Triolian became a favorite of blues players.

1930 National Style O

In 1930, National split the difference between its expensive tricone models and its more affordable single-cones with the introduction of the Style O. After an initial run with a steel body, National changed the Style O to a nickel-plated bell brass body that produced a richer, more elegant tone than the steel-bodied single-cones. Its etched Hawaiian imagery gave it an elegant look as well. At $85, it was $40 less than the cheapest tricone. The combination of tone, looks, and affordability made the Style O one of National's most popular models.

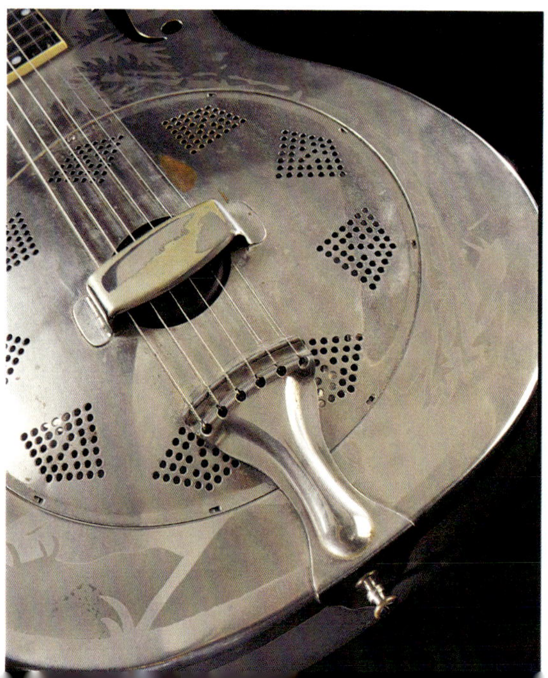

Tommy Comeaux was a pivotal figure in the Louisiana music scene that I stepped into in the early 1990s. His generosity of spirit and musicality, along with the fact that he was capable of holding that role while simultaneously maintaining a full-time career as a doctor, made him an inspiration to many. When I met someone locally they'd ask me first if I knew Tommy. When I was at a festival in Colorado or Rhode Island and met a bluegrasser or folk musician and told them that I lived in Lafayette, they'd ask me first if I knew Tommy. He had that kind of presence, and his love for the music was often expressed in his commitment to acquiring and playing the most beautiful instruments he could find.

In the mid-1990s, my wife Christine Balfa and I had quite a few musical friends from both out of town and out of the country coming to stay at our home. We were in our 20s, and our place on Bayou Teche was often full of visitors playing music at all hours of the night. A friend from England, a great musician, came over to stay with us for a few weeks.

Not long before the end of his scheduled trip, he fell head-over-heels in love with a Cajun gal. In a side note that still makes me laugh, he felt sure they were going to consummate this new relationship during a drive around the very remote shores of Lake Martin. She stopped her car somewhere along the lake's gravel road and asked him, "Do you want to get down?" In southwest Louisiana that means "Do you want to get out of the car," because in the not-too-distant past, the Cajun French verb *descender* got into English as "get down," which is literally how you reach the ground from a buggy. But in most English-speaking parts of the world it means something else! So you can imagine what was going through my friend's head. He was thinking about "getting down" in a much more exciting context . . . and of course the eagerness in his eyes conveyed "Hell yes, I want to get down!!" But then she opened the door, got out—down—and walked to the lake. It wasn't quite the getting down he had envisioned, not by a long shot, but rather a sublime moment in the "two peoples divided by a common language" historical phenomenon.

My love-afflicted friend was desperate to change his departure date and stay longer. On the day before he was due to fly home, he called the airline inquiring about a change, but they told him that he could extend his ticket only with a doctor's excuse. Christine and I wondered if we might actually be able to make that happen and . . . Tommy! So we introduced him to our lovesick friend. And Tommy, with a wink and a smile and a knowing nod, wrote him an official excuse, saying that he was unable to fly, thereby giving these lovers a few more days together. I can still see his smile as he handed over the note . . . ahhhh, young love . . .

Tommy did what he could do. Could he have lost his medical license for this blatant falsehood? Or is lovesickness a legitimate disease? I don't know, but I do know that one of the blessings of music is the paths that cross because of it. Seeing my friend's bright, hopeful eyes and energized heart, Tommy recognized the good for what it was and the special moments we will look back on later in life if we are blessed enough to get there. He chose to create a moment in which love won. It's still a deep loss that Tommy didn't get to arrive at that distant point where he could have looked back at a long life full of those moments and connections. But so many people here have been willing to do it for him and still are. That says more than anything about the power of who he was and how he touched the lives of many.

—DIRK POWELL

1990
Dobro
Presentation

Outlandish! But this koa wood dobro (the brand's name became a blanket term for all resonators) is as is as functional as it is beautiful. It was constructed for the 1994 NAMM show, hence the "Presentation" designation. Profusely inlaid, it is one of a kind. It was acquired by Tommy from Elderly Instruments in 1997, and is now in the hands of a private collector in Ohio.

The Comeaux Family Special Collection

1921 Gibson mandolin Style A-2

Orville Gibson's sole patent was for a mandolin with its top and back carved into an arched shape. With the heavy promotional efforts of the Gibson company, founded in 1902, along with Gibson's network of teacher-agents, the Gibson carved-top style soon dominated the mandolin world. In the 1910s, at the height of the mandolin's popularity, Gibson offered two fancy, scroll-body F-style models as well as five different versions of the symmetrical Style A, with the A-2 in the middle of the line. One hundred-plus years later, Gibson Style A mandolins are still viable for modern playing styles.

1915
Gibson Style U Harp

Gibson touted the harp guitar as the next step in the evolution of the guitar. And in theory, it was. The rack of "sub-bass" strings provided guitarists with the richness of lower bass notes for a deeper harmonic reach. But in reality, the right-hand technique required more effort to master than most guitarists were willing to invest. Also, the size of the instrument made it unwieldy—to carry around as well as to play. Although Gibson devoted the center spread of its catalogs to the harp guitar well into the 1930s, it never caught on.

1997 Gilchrist Mandolin 4 Custom

Gibson's earliest mandolins inspired Tommy to commission this ornate instrument from Australian maker Stephen Gilchrist. The alternating abalone and mother-of-pearl top border appeared only on Gibson's F-4—the top model in the early years—and only in Gibson's first catalog, published in 1903. The tortoiseshell pickguard inlaid into the top is another feature of early Gibson mandolins. The elaborate, intricate fingerboard inlay was not a standard Gibson spec but was found on the occasional "presentation" or "artist" mandolin, designed to show off the maker's art or as a special ornament for an artist.

1990 Gilchrists

Stephen Gilchrist began making mandolins in Warnambool, Australia, in 1975. In 1980, after building eighty instruments, he spent a year in Nashville working in the repair shop of Gruhn Guitars, a prominent vintage dealer. There he could study and work on the legendary Gibson mandolins signed by acoustic engineer Lloyd Loar from 1922–24. He returned to Australia inspired, and began building mandolins in the traditional Gibson style. In an era when Gibson's quality had fallen, he quickly gained a reputation as the world's finest traditional-style luthier for the mandolin family—a reputation that continues today. The majority of Gilchrists feature the dusky brown "Cremona sunburst" finish of the Loar-signed Gibsons from the 1920s. The natural-finish mandolin features the same elaborate fingerboard inlay as an early Gibson F-4 Artist.

1960
Gretsch
6120 Chet Atkins

In 1954, the Gretsch company of Brooklyn, New York, designed a new model with up-and-coming Nashville guitarist Chet Atkins. The Chet Atkins Hollow Body (Model 6120) was the first of six Gretsch models to bear Atkins's name. It would become Gretsch's most famous and most enduring model, used by rock 'n' rollers of the late 1950s, such as rockabilly singer Eddie Cochran and "twangy" instrumentalist Duane Eddy, and neo-rockabilly Brian Setzer with the Stray Cats in the 1980s and up to the present day.

1962 Gibson ES-335 TDC

By the mid-1950s, most electric guitarists fell into two camps: those who preferred the modern body shape and sustaining power of a solid-body guitar, and those who preferred the more subdued tones of a traditional hollow body. In 1958, Gibson president Ted McCarty brought the two together by inventing the semi-hollow-body guitar. The ES-335 had the arched top and F-holes that went back to the earliest electrics, but with a modern double-cutaway body with a center block to make it perform like a solid body. The ES-335 was a success from its introduction, and it has never gone out of production.

1993
PAUL REED SMITH
DRAGON #17

Paul Reed Smith of Annapolis, Maryland, launched his guitar company in 1985 and immediately gained recognition for his elegant design elements, including highly figured "10 tops" and flying bird fingerboard inlays. Seven years later, he celebrated the growing popularity of PRS guitars with a limited run of fifty instruments featuring an elaborate dragon figure inlaid on the fingerboard as well as a new pickup design. The PRS Dragons were so popular that versions II and III followed in 1993 and 1994. This is No. 17 of the run of one hundred Dragons in 1993.

Gibson SJN Country Western

Gibson broke away from its model numbering system in the 1930s with a large-bodied "dreadnought" guitar called simply the Jumbo. During World War II, Gibson's southeastern sales representative, Tom Peacock, suggested a model for his customers that would feature double parallelogram fingerboard inlays and a traditional sunburst finish. It was called the Southern Jumbo, and it was immediately successful all over the country. In 1955, Gibson once again created a new name to call attention to a model variation. The SJN was the natural-finish version of the SJ, but Gibson tied it to an up-and-coming musical genre and named it the Country Western.

Collings Tree of Life Guitar

Bill Collings of Austin, Texas, built his reputation on guitars inspired by the classic flat-top models of Martin and Gibson. The size and the body lines of this guitar are recognizable as Martin's OM (Orchestra Model) or OOO-size. The intricate Tree of Life fingerboard inlay is found on many fancy instruments of the early twentieth century, although it is rarely seen on a Collings guitar. After establishing himself as one of the leading makers of flat-tops, Collings expanded into archtop guitars, electric guitars, mandolins, traditional guitar cases, and a modern interpretation of the lightly built, inexpensive guitars of the 1930s.

1990 Gilchrist Archtop Guitar

The Gibson company initially viewed the guitar as an extension of the mandolin family, so it's no surprise that renowned Australian mandolin maker Stephen Gilchrist should also be one of the most highly respected makers of archtop guitars. As he does with mandolins, Gilchrist typically follows the classic designs of Gibson's L-5 and Super 400, elements of which include the pointed fingerboard end, the Y-shaped tailpiece, and the highly figured maple neck and back. The chevron or "tweed" inlays are Gilchrist's design. This 17-inch guitar was one of four instruments that Tommy ordered directly from Gilchrist.

CA. 1870
Honoré Derazey Violin

"Head fiddles" are a tribute to sixteenth-century luthier Gaspard Duiffopruggcar, whose bearded head adorns this violin's scroll. Also typical are the castle scene on the back and the Latin inscription on the rims, which is written from the point of view of the wood. It translates as "I was living in the forest; the cruel ax did slay me. Living, I was mute; dead, I sweetly sing." This head fiddle is attributed to violin maker Honoré Derazey of Mirecourt, France, whose reputation today is based in part on his copies of Duiffopruggcar violins.

FACIEBAT ANNO 17 VIOLIN

This well-worn violin has passed through the hands Tommy Comeaux's bandmates over the last two decades and is still out there making music. It was made in Germany in the late 1800s, and the label inside the instrument reads "Antonius Stradivarius Cremonensis; Faciebat Anno 17." This common appearance of the Stradivari name merely means "in the style of" the great builder from the early 1700s in Cremona, Italy. The true value of this instrument is how it feels and sounds to the player.

1915
Gibson H-4 Mandola

Competing with established makers in much larger cities, the Gibson Mandolin-Guitar Mfg. Co. of Kalamazoo, Michigan, rose to the top by promoting mandolin groups, with music and instruments modeled on the string quartet elements of first and second violin, viola, and cello. In keeping with the relationship between violin and viola, the mandola was larger than a mandolin and tuned the same as a viola. With this design, string quartet arrangements could be easily adapted for mandolin quartets and orchestras. The H-4 was the top mandola model in the Gibson line of the 1910s. In 1915, when this instrument was made, the H-4 listed for $125.

Monteleone Grand Artist Mandolin

John Monteleone first made his mark in the 1970s as a maker of mandolins in the style of Gibson's classic F-5. He soon introduced his own design elements, as seen on this Grand Artist model that features a more relaxed scroll, streamlined pickguard, a fingerboard extension, and a larger, flared headstock shape. By the 1990s, his archtop guitars were gaining recognition for their imaginative aesthetics. In 2011, when the Metropolitan Museum of Art curated the Guitar Heroes exhibit, Monteleone was included with two other Italian-American guitar makers, John D'Angelico and James D'Aquisto.

Gibson Melody Maker

Gibson's reputation is based on its most expensive models, but its sales leaders have typically been the most affordable models. By the late 1950s, the single-pickup Les Paul Junior was outselling all the other Les Pauls, but Gibson aimed for a wider market at a lower price point with the Melody Maker. Cost-saving features included a thinner body, narrower headstock, and a self-contained pickup/pickguard/control assembly. The single-pickup version listed for $99.50 compared to $132.50 for the Les Paul Junior. And for only $2.50 more than the single-pickup Junior, a guitarist could get a two-pickup Melody Maker.

Tommy Comeaux

Medicine Man

BY DAVE HUSSONG

There were no strangers in Tommy Comeaux's life. He moved effortlessly through the most demanding of personalities as well as careers. Creative and rational, music and medicine, from consummate artist to pathologist, he created community wherever he went. There are few individuals who possess the talent and intellect, and to a degree, the sense of timing needed to develop the success that Tommy was beginning to enjoy. He's been called an enigma. I believe he was the quintessential Renaissance man—it's an overused term, but correct in Tommy's case. If it was a positive endeavor, Tommy was there. "If there's anything else I can do for you, just let me know" was one of his oft-used phrases. And he meant it.

Tommy was considered to be one of the most versatile Cajun musicians, being adept at a number of different stringed instruments, with his focus being dobro, mandolin, and bass. His diversity and skill on those instruments led to him being nominated for and winning the title of Best Cajun Guitarist in a 1995 Louisiana music poll. It was a title of which he was particularly proud because he always considered himself a team player rather than a soloist. For an example of Tommy's work, check out his guitar solo on "Balfa et Grand Bois" on Coteau's 1997 Rounder Records release, *Highly Seasoned Cajun Music*.

His tenure with America's premier Cajun band, BeauSoleil, extends back more than twenty years. With that group he was nominated for a Grammy on four different occasions. Tommy's multi-instrumental work is beautifully preserved on BeauSoleil's 1995 live release, *Vintage BeauSoleil*, recorded for the Music of the World label. Along with BeauSoleil leader Michael Doucet, he recorded as well a soundtrack for NPR's Rabbit Ears Radio entitled *The Talking Eggs*, narrated by Sissy Spacek. Also, as testimony to his diversity, a Comeaux guitar track recorded for a new theme for an ABC affiliate in Louisiana is still being aired today. Along with his involvement in BeauSoleil, and more

recently Coteau, Tommy was also an active participant in two regional favorites, the Basin Brothers and the Clickin' Chickens. Friend, fellow bandmate, and contemporary slide master Sonny Landreth was quoted as saying, "Tommy was the best of the best." Landreth went on the say, "Cajun-born and Cajun-bred, Tommy personified the *joie de vivre* of the native culture." Comeaux's wellspring of creativity, influence, and personal warmth seemed to be without limits.

Over the past decade, the good doctor had become well known in the vintage instrument community through his acquisition of what had become a world-class collection of stringed instruments. His interests were as diverse as his own personality—from Lloyd Loar-period guitars and mandolins, to Fender Stratocasters made from 1966 to 1970—the Hendrix period, as he would refer to it. "Dave, a lot of people don't realize that Hendrix did the majority of his truly influential work on late '60s CBS instruments, not the older stuff," he told me on more than one occasion, and of course he was right. The 1966 Stratocasters have some of the finest necks that ever came from the Fender Company before or after the 1965 sale of Leo Fender's company to CBS.

The Clickin' Chickens, from left: Gary Newman, Ben Shank, Carl Brown, Steve Schneider, Tommy Comeaux, Phil Schneider

Tommy was valedictorian of his senior high school class. He then graduated summa cum laude from Louisiana State University and later Alpha Omega Alpha from LSU Medical School. After serving his residency in New Orleans, Tommy returned to Lafayette to become resident pathologist at Our Lady Of Lourdes Medical Center, later becoming head of that department.

Despite the time involved with his music and his day job, Tommy was a dedicated and lifelong fitness junkie, winning awards as a marathon runner. He had recently taken up bicycling, and it was during a morning ride on Saturday, November 8, 1997 that he was struck on a residential street by a driver who had apparently suffered an epileptic seizure. Tommy Comeaux died instantly.

In a conversation with his mother, Dorinne "Candy" Comeaux, shortly after his passing, she pointed out to me with great pride that her son was also a lay minister in his church.

From left: Tommy Comeaux, guitar; Al Berard, mandolin; Keith Blanchard, drums; Warren Zevon, guitar; Errol Verret, accordion. 1995

A benefit celebrating Tommy Comeaux's spirit and memory was held on December 26th of that year at Grant Street Dance Hall in Lafayette. It featured performances from many of the bands that Tommy had been associated with through the years, including Native Sons, Clicken' Chickens, the Basin Brothers, Coteau, BeauSoleil, and Sonny Landreth. Titled "Medicine Show," the proceeds went to the Dr. Tommy Comeaux Memorial Fund.

To this writer, Tommy Comeaux possessed a range of consciousness that was rare, if not unique. He didn't talk about it, it wasn't something he stumbled upon at sunrise now and then; it was abiding and rational, and he employed it day in and day out. It was his gift, and he used it to pursue the most ethereal of goals: the helping of his fellow man. He was truly highly evolved, and he made a profound difference in many people's lives at many levels and in many different circles. He certainly made a

HONORS

1970 High School Class Valedictorian
Rensselaer Polytechnic Institute Mathematics and Science Award
American Legion Award
Optimist Junior Citizen Medal

1973 Valedictorian, Louisiana State University and A&M College
Mu Sigma Rho Fraternity Honorary Scholastic Attainment, Louisiana State University
Louisiana State University Chapter of Phi Kappa Phi Honor Society

1977 Graduated LSU School of Medicine

1982-1997 Member, American Board of Pathology
Pathology Continuing Medical Educational Award: American Society for Clinical Pathology, College of American Pathologists, United States and Canadian Academy of Pathology, and the Intersociety Pathology Council
American Medical Association Physician's Recognition Award
Fellow in the College of American Pathologists

1985 Grammy Nomination

1987 Grammy Nomination

1989 Grammy Nomination

1991 Grammy Nomination

1992 Member, Louisiana Music Commission
Board Member, National Academy of Recording Arts & Sciences

1994 Grammy Award: Best Traditional Folk Album, BeauSoleil, *L'Echo*

1997 Grammy Award: Best Traditional Folk Album, BeauSoleil, *L'Amour Ou La Folie*

1998 Thomas G. Comeaux, M.D. Annual Premedical Scholarship at the Univeristy of Southwestern Louisiana named by the Lafayette Parish Medical Society

2011 Dr. Tommy Comeaux Endowed Chair in Traditional Music established at University of Louisiana at Lafayette

difference in mine, and I never met him in person. I can only imagine the privilege to have been his lifelong friend. I'll close this tribute with some thoughts on Tommy sent to me by a man who was indeed his lifelong friend, Michael Doucet:

> Dear David,
> Here are a few thoughts about Tommy Comeaux.
>
> Until his recent, untimely death, Tommy Comeaux was the oldest and closest friend I had. Our mutual love of music included playing together in numerous groups and configurations since the mid-1960s, including BeauSoleil recordings from 1977 to the present, as well as many hours spent simply jamming and talking. Since 1982, when Tommy took a position with a local pathology group, his day job has afforded him the necessary funds to begin appeasing his passion for collecting excellent, high quality vintage instruments. His collection included over 200 guitars, mandolins, and amplifiers. From his first Yamaha acoustic that he played throughout his high school, college, and med school years to his most recent acquisition, a Lloyd Loar L5, all instruments were kept in view at his house and played at least once a month. The following was a typical Tommy phone call:
>
> TC: "Hey man, there's something burning down my house!"
> MD: "Oh yeah! What did you get this time? Does it have eight or six strings?"
> TC: "Can't tell you over the phone, you've got to come over for a couple of minutes and jam."
>
> His strings are silent now but his generosity and friendship endure.
>
> —Michael Doucet, BeauSoleil

February 1998

A life becomes a legacy

Tommy Comeaux (1952–1997)

TODD MOUTON

Even decades later, Tommy Comeaux could still play the songs from his high school rock band, the Null Set. "Tommy had an amazing memory," explains Grammy-nominated bandleader Sonny Landreth, who was part of those school auditorium gigs but today is admittedly a little rusty on the finer points of the budding band's arrangements.

The two musicians met as Lafayette High School students in the late 1960s, and their friendship grew over the ensuing years through intertwining projects graced by Tommy's seemingly boundless generosity. "He was truly interested in other people," Sonny adds. "I've never seen anything like it. He wouldn't just take you in, he'd take you and your whole family in."

The musician, physician, and humanitarian made you feel that you were the sole focus of his attention when you spoke with him. When he died tragically in a bicycling accident in November 1997, his loss tore a gaping hole in the region's social and cultural fabric. Friends from music, medicine, and many other fields gathered to imagine appropriate tributes, only to encounter the ripple effects of Tommy's life and work bouncing back from distant shores.

The diverse group that would become known as the Comeauxtians soon came up with a concept that united and added new dimensions to Tommy's impressive achievements in music and academia. A drive to establish a ground-breaking million dollar endowment for a traditional music program was launched, and over the course of numerous special events, worldwide radio broadcasts, album releases and more, hundreds of donors from around the globe united to meet, then exceed that initial goal. And contributions keep coming in.

The University of Louisiana at Lafayette's innovative traditional music program named in Tommy's honor is now thriving. There are now many other tangible tributes to Tommy's memory, including an elegant bicycle rest stop on Bayou Tortue Road in Broussard, and a plaque at the Acadiana Park Nature Station in Lafayette commemorating his work as a conservationist. The series of live recordings produced from the Medicine Show fundraiser concerts have showcased a wide range of tribute performances, including the song "Quiet Man" by Native Sons. Tommy last performed with that band the night before he died, and their elegiac composition debuted onstage just weeks later.

During Tommy's life, he paid tribute to the talents of others by loaning instruments from his staggering personal collection to artists including Mark Knopfler and Derek Trucks when they were recording in the area. And now the tributes return to him. Bandleader Jerry Douglas closed his 1998 album *Restless On The Farm* with his composition "For Those Who've Gone Clear" dedicated to the memory of Tommy and other departed friends. "Chanson Pour Tommy," another original instrumental tribute, graces BeauSoleil's 1999 *Cajunization* album. Some of Tommy's home recording gear became part of renowned south Louisiana audio engineer and

producer Tony Daigle's studio in Lafayette, which bears the name Electric Comoland in tribute. Numerous Grammy-nominated and Grammy-winning projects now list that credit, and some of Tommy's other possessions played a role in the successful development of Riverfront Music and Komet Amplifiers across the swamp in Baton Rouge.

"Looking back on it, I don't know how he had the time and energy to keep up with all that," Landreth says, describing Tommy's many interests and pursuits. "I think it all comes back to he just genuinely cared about people, and that motivated him to do so much for so many."

Tommy was a Renaissance man during a time of cultural rebirth in south Louisiana, and he found a place for himself just outside the spotlight. Though he was a member of a half-dozen bands at the time of his passing, he was never a frontman, and his offstage accomplishments were also marked by humility.

"He touched so many lives, in a personal way, on a really profound level, and you can see how that's grown," Landreth adds. Tommy was soft-spoken and supportive, and the notion that his example will inspire future generations is perhaps the greatest tribute possible for this man for all seasons.

Quiet Man

How they come, how they come
to take, to take another walk with you
and to stand next to your soothing grace
Lord, the sky's never been so blue

Clouds a-passing, everchanging where we stand
I hear chimes a-ringing from the hands of a quiet man

Oh to walk, oh to walk with you
gentle steps touching down
and to reach, oh to reach like you
your sweet blessings spreading 'round

Oh this bitter fruit, we yearn to understand
I can feel the healing from the hands of a quiet man

How they cry, oh to cry with you
sweet release rolling down
and to laugh, oh to laugh with you
precious moments forever found

Melodies arising, another soul slips from our hands
I hear chimes a-ringing from the heart of a quiet man

Dance on the horizon
aren't they glad they came
melodies arising
hear the band play

Hear the band play, Lord
hear the band play
dance on the horizon
hear the band play

DANNY KIMBALL–MIKE HANISEE

DR. TOMMY COMEAUX ENDOWED CHAIR IN TRADITIONAL MUSIC AT THE UNIVERSITY OF LOUISIANA AT LAFAYETTE

DR. MARK DeWITT

Above: Aaron Barilleaux plays with the acoustic blues ensemble, April 2018. Right: Vermilion Express performs its November 2017 bluegrass concert (l-r): Luke Huval, fiddle; Celebrindal Roberts, mandolin; Emily Ortego, guitar; Len Springer, bass; Lakeyn Schultz, guitar; Benjamin Richey, banjo.

I realized when I was hired in 2010 that the work of building a traditional music program from the ground up would be an awesome responsibility and opportunity, and potentially a lot of fun. All of that has proven to be the case, and beyond. It took a few years to plan and develop the basic ingredients of the program: applied music instruction in an oral tradition (how to play and sing), ensembles (bands for credit), a songwriting class, music appreciation classes, a BA degree concentration in traditional music, and guest artists. We now strive to fill out the program with the kinds of offerings that attract students and to apply lessons learned. Interest income from the endowment has provided a stable budget for programming and hiring traditional musicians from the community as adjunct instructors to provide practical instruction.

In the spring of 2011, we hired our first adjunct instructor in traditional music, Wilson Savoy, to teach a Cajun band class. Only a few years before as a student, Wilson and some other members of what was to become the Pine Leaf Boys had been told they could not play Cajun music in public on campus, and so it was with great relish that we started reversing that trend with Wilson's help. The following school year, Wilson started teaching private accordion lessons for credit, and we hired David Greely (who had recently retired from performing

Above: Dr. Chad Huval leads an all-star instructor band at the Blue Moon Saloon, off campus, December 2018.

with the Steve Riley and the Mamou Playboys, the band he co-founded with Riley) to teach fiddle. Other hires followed in short order: Kristi Guillory to teach a beginning accordion class, Al Berard to teach a fiddle class. It has been a privilege to work with these and other bright lights of Cajun and zydeco music who have served on our faculty over the years: Sam Broussard, Megan Brown Constantin, Brazos Huval, Chad Huval, Kelli Jones, Yvette Landry, Corey Ledet, Mitch Reed, Roddie Romero, Drew Simon, Nathan Williams Jr., Kevin Wimmer, and Lee Allen Zeno.

While Tommy Comeaux did play for quite a few years with BeauSoleil, his friends were quick to remind me that Tommy's musical tastes ventured far beyond Cajun music, and so even before we offered a zydeco band for credit (the Ragin' Steppers, taught by Nathan Williams Jr. aka Lil Nate), we started a bluegrass band that we named Vermilion Express. Dr. Len Springer, a member of the fundraising group and one-time Nashville fiddler, developed and has taught the class for five years now. A couple of years later, we added the Ragin' Blues Band, an electric lineup first led by Corey Ledet that enjoyed a guest sit-in from Sonny Landreth on their first concert. Student interest in the blues was strong enough that now we also have the Royal Roots Blues Band, an acoustic outfit led by Marty Christian.

Likewise, our guest artists over the years have been a welcome mixture of the best in Louisiana French music and a variety of other genres from around the nation and the world. In the program's first year (2010-11), BeauSoleil avec Michael Doucet were artists-in-residence celebrating their thirty-fifth anniversary as a band, and they were presented with the SPARK Lifetime Achievement Award in the Arts from the College of the Arts. Three years later, Steve Riley and the Mamou Playboys came to campus to celebrate their twenty-fifth anniversary, visited classes, and played a memorable concert with the UL Lafayette Symphony.

Top: Wilson Savoy (at right) conducts his "front porch final" outside of Angelle Hall at the end of our Cajun ensemble's first semester. L-r: Dane Thibodeaux, Jo Vidrine, Lance Boston, Danny Devillier. Bottom: Acoustic blues ensemble performs at university's observance of Fête de la terre (Earth Day), April 2018 (l-r): Sarah Rumsey, Joe Harper, Aaron Barrilleaux, Devin Sonnier, Nicole Needham, Hayden Bogard.

Top left: Sonny Landreth (at left) rehearses with Ragin' Blues Band, March 2016 (l-r): Myles Migl, Joe Harper, Dakota Pique, Trevor Lee. Bottom left: Forest Huval and Michael Doucet jam inside the BeauSoleil Louisiana Solar Home, February 2011.

In 2016, folklorist and radio host Nick Spitzer received his SPARK award and emceed a zydeco dance party onstage in the Angelle Hall auditorium with Lawrence Ardoin and Geno Delafose. We have hosted other guests representing bluegrass (Alecia Nugent, Peter Rowan), Irish (the Brock McGuire Band), jazz (Irvin Mayfield, Laurie Antonioli), and Hungarian folk traditions.

Our student bands have had a wide variety of performance opportunities over the years both on and off campus: homecoming events at the Alumni Center, jamming on the first day of classes in front of the library or at the Student Union, academic convocation, playing for dancers at the Blue Moon Saloon, visiting area schools, leading jams at Festivals Acadiens et Créoles, and performing on the Louisiana Folk Roots stage at Festival International de Louisiane, to name a few examples. Vermilion Express has even ventured out of state, first to the Bloomin' Bluegrass Festival in Farmers Branch, Texas, to test their jamming skills in 2017, and the following year to the International Bluegrass Music Association's annual meeting in Raleigh, North Carolina, where they met with other college bluegrass bands, and followed that with a set at the World of Bluegrass Festival in downtown Raleigh.

One key aspect of any musical tradition is creativity. To that end, we added a songwriting class to the curriculum early on. In the first offering, we invited four Lafayette-based songwriters to visit the class multiple times, culminating in a semester-ending songwriter showcase in Burke-Hawthorne Hall featuring each student in the class alongside Yvette Landry, Sam Broussard, Nathan Williams Sr., and

Below: The Ragin' Blues Band plays an off-campus gig at Artmosphere in Lafayette, November 2016 (l-r): Abner Rodriguez, Nick Tanner, Kayla Dugas, Joe Harper.

Above: The Angelle Aces lead a Cajun jam at Festivals Acadiens et Créoles, October 2018: Julie Babineaux, guitar; Gracie Babineaux, accordion.

the late David Egan. Since then we have offered the class once a year, taught in succession by Yvette Landry, Johanna Divine, Kelli Jones, Sam Broussard, and Gordon Bradberry.

The mission of the Dr. Tommy Comeaux Endowed Chair in Traditional Music is to stimulate interdisciplinary research on the foundations and diversity of traditional music worldwide and to advance the preservation, instruction, and performance of traditional music with an emphasis on traditions that have developed in Acadiana, Louisiana's French-influenced southern parishes. While we have obviously been busy offering instruction and programming performances, we have also pursued the research side. I have presented papers at conferences and published book chapters on topics including the Cajun accordion as an identity symbol, the range of traditional music programs in North America analogous to ours, and environmental protest songs in Louisiana. I have been active as a research fellow at the Center for Louisiana Studies, depositing field and concert recordings in their archives and partnering with them on projects, including Festivals Acadiens et Creoles' fortieth anniversary (2014), and constructing a digital humanities platform connecting francophone archives in France, Canada, and Louisiana hosted by Université Poitiers in France.

Some of our graduate students developed research interests in traditional music while studying here; I have supervised master's theses on Pentecostal gospel music, Nicaraguan folk music, the impact of amplification on zydeco music, and Cajun music in the classroom. Marie-Laure Boudreau, a recent PhD in Francophone Studies and longtime accordion student with us, wrote her dissertation (in French) on the impact of the internet in the transmission of Cajun and Creole music.

In keeping with the mission of research on "traditional music worldwide," I have from time to time offered a graduate seminar in ethnomusicology and an undergraduate class in the appreciation of world music. I have worked with our percussion department and the Ryan School of Irish Dance in Lafayette to give world music students the experience of playing a set of Javanese gamelan instruments or West African drums, or of ceilidh dancing to Irish music. Jessamyn Doan, an ethnomusicologist who wrote her dissertation on Cajun music for the

Top right: Traditional music major Randall Jackson demonstrates his piano accordion to pupils at Myrtle Elementary School in Lafayette, February 2016. Bottom right: Myrtle Elementary's French immersion music teacher, Jimmy Louis-Marie (left), assists with a clinic given to faculty member Troy Breaux (right) and his percussion ensemble, on the eve of Dédé St. Prix's appearance at Festival International de Louisiane, 2016.

Top left: Percussion ensemble with guest teacher Midiyanto (sixth from left) after playing their first concert dedicated solely to central Javanese gamelan, February 2018. Bottom left: Members of the acoustic blues ensemble, April 2018 (l-r): Hayden Bogard (bass), Sarah Rumsey (tenor), Nicole Needham (lead), Mark DeWitt (baritone, instructor).

University of Pennsylvania and worked on the advising staff of our university, also taught the class a couple of times. Guest artists we have brought in for world music instruction include gamelan master Midiyanto, Paul Brock and his fellow Irish bandmates, folk music student-musicians from Brittany, and Martinican percussion master Dédé St. Prix, who was here in Lafayette to perform at Festival International.

The School of Music obtained approval to offer bachelor of arts degrees in both music business and traditional music in the same year. Since then, music business students have been an integral part of the traditional music program, most often as performers but also helping occasionally with event publicity, at the soundboard, or in the recording booth. For example, recent music business graduate Nick Tanner played electric bass and guitar with the Ragin' Blues Band, engineered and mixed the first recordings that our acoustic blues ensemble made, and interned with Festival International and at the famed Dockside Studio. Lakeyn Schultz, another music business graduate, honed her craft in our bluegrass band, did her internship in Nashville, and now lives and works in that city. Ailee Pardi, a student of Cajun fiddle and vocals who earned our first-ever degree in traditional music, returned to the West Coast following graduation to work and prepare for graduate school. Recently, students have been applying to some of our other degree concentrations (BM in Music Media, MM in Performance) with the intention of studying traditional music on their major instrument.

In short, Tommy Comeaux's legacy on the UL Lafayette campus is to bring some of the finest musicians from this community's deep talent pool to our campus week in, week out, and to open our students' eyes to the rich history of traditional music, its worldwide reach, and its relevance for the future.

June 2019

Below: Graduate student Kylie Veazey leads the Zydeco Ragin' Steppers at the Blue Moon Saloon, December 2018.

Top left: Sonny Landreth performs with the Ragin' Blues Band, April 2016 (l-r): Joe Harper, Landreth, Myles Migl, Trevor Lee, Mark St. Cyr. Bottom left: Nick Tanner levitating on bass with the Ragin' Blues Band at the Blue Moon Saloon, December 2016. Bottom center: Brayden Chase Moore and Randall Jackson perform with the Zydeco Ragin' Steppers at the Blue Moon Saloon, December 2016. Above: Hunter Hebert on sax for the Ragin' Blues Band while vocalist Yanni Richard (background) appreciates, April 2019.

ABOUT THE AUTHOR

David 'Shakin' Dave' Hussong, graduate of Dayton Art Institute, and alumnus of Antioch University Midwest, has spent his career developing his guitar-related business interests. Initially working with award-winning designer J. Raymond Davis, then gravitating to regional guitar and vocal work, he caught "the infamous train to Chicago," landed a gig with the band Selah, and booked through Baby Huey's agent at Pillar Artists. The results were bookings around Chicago and on up to Wisconsin and Michigan, and fifty years later he's still under their contract. On returning to Dayton (one of the seven cosmic centers of the universe!), he launched Fretware Guitar, what he refers to as "a movement" to unearth the rarest fretted instruments. Beginning with Dan Armstrong on La Guardia Place, then working with George Gruhn on 4th Avenue North, he then worked alongside Jay Scott, thereby deepening his knowledge of the vintage instrument business. Performances in Dallas led to a "right place, right time" relationship with Charlie's Guitars, allowing him a rubbing of elbows, which led to Fretware Guitars emerging as one of the top ten vintage instrument sources in the nation. During the 1990s, a prosperous time for vintage instrument collecting, he began writing regularly for *Vintage Guitar Magazine*. And a thirty-seven-year stretch at WYSO as host of "Shakin' Dave Hussong's Hall of Fame Blues" put vintage sounds on the airwaves. Vintage instruments on stage, on air, and in print put him before collectors, which is how he met Dr. Tommy Comeaux, an individual who left such an indelible mark on so many. Honored to have created this tribute to Tommy, Hussong notes, "You attain a certain chronological plateau and realize that memorable experiences all seem to fall into the past-tense category. This multimedia salute to an exceptional, multi-gifted human being after twenty-three years is still perfectly placed. God bless you Tommy!"

ABOUT THE PHOTOGRAPHER

Jim France is a commercial photographer working in Naples, Florida, and Colombia, South America. To capture the full beauty of these instruments he shot with a Mamiya RB67 camera in 2 1/4" by 2 3/4" film format with Norman P2000 strobe lights, with 22" beauty dish, a 36" soft box and a 6" freznel spotlight.

Jim recalls, "Dave contacted me by phone and wanted me to photograph a collection of guitars he had recently acquired. I was not familiar with Tommy Comeaux and was not a musician but I certainly wanted to do the work. Some days later he brought the instruments and we spread them out on the studio floor. My jaw dropped. I saw exquisite pieces of art with their lines, curves, wear, details, and they amazed me!

"The following session we shot on the floor of Dave's store in Franklin, Ohio, formerly a historic bank. I'll never forget him opening the vault in the basement and seeing it filled with fretted instruments.

"Dave's dream from the beginning was that this collection be published in book form. I am so glad that after all these years his vision is coming to light. I am proud to have been a part of it."

ACKNOWLEDGMENTS

Thank You Dr. Walter and Candy Comeaux for their faith in me. Ira Stanley, "Mr. 335" and a brother, who was beyond imperative to the construction of this memorial to Tommy Comeaux; Steve and Dayan Harlamert, absolute gems in my life; Mr. Bill Archer, Jose Higgins, and the late Jim Roberts, traveling partners and compadres, God bless; Michael Cox, "Mr. Good Balance"; F. M. Achor and Dr. Ken Engebretson; Alan Greenwood and the late Jeanine Shea of *Vintage Guitar Magazine*; my fretted instrument guru; Mark Kaiser, I'm lost without you bro; Rebecca S. Hussong, my forever partner and love, thanks for tolerating me; Professor John "Toad" Hussong, who started and inspired me on this adventure so long ago and continues to be an inspiration; Amanda Hussong Cox, my in-house editor, "So Proud Being Loved by You"; Griffin David Hussong, my ultimate upright bassist and salsa king; Tim Coy, "Mr. Put A Price On It!" at Centerville Music; Derek Johnson, my best man, "the proof is in the details"; Todd Ostendorf, award-winning artist-designer in Dayton who originally laid out this tribute; and lastly, Niki and all my cohorts in crime at WYSO for allowing me thirty-seven years to give an aural voice to these instruments, whether in the hands of Tommy Comeaux, B. B. King, Otis Rush, J. G. Watson, Duke Robillard, Junior Watson, the Vaughn Brothers, Sleepy Reed Haas, Anson Funderburgh, or Oscar Moore. Each of these individuals is a "forever" influence and realizes without question that the pecking order could never be properly ordered. I thank you all for your love and giving aid to my complexity—well okay, my lack of rationalization—okay, okay—my ability to organize! You all have made invaluable contributions to Shakin' Dave's learning process, and God willing it's not all in the past tense! Thank you!

CONTRIBUTORS

Sam Broussard, Editor
Derek Johnson
Walter Carter
Laurence Wexer
Todd Mouton
Dr. Mark DeWitt, Dr. Tommy Comeaux Endowed Chair for Traditional Music
Steve Conn
Michael Doucet
Jerry Douglas
Eric Johnson
Sonny Landreth
Patrick Mould
Gary Newman
Tim O'Brien
Dirk Powell

PHOTOGRAPHY CREDITS

Jim France, cover, pages 1-105
Valerie Brazeale, page 127
Don Bertrand, pages 97, 107, 131
Clark Comeaux, pages 110, 114, 116, 129
Mark DeWitt, pages 135-138
Courtesy of Michael Doucet, page 65
Terri Fensel for UL Lafayette, pages 134, 135, 138, 139
Travis Gauthier, pages 111-113, 115, 117-122
Catherine Guidry for UL Lafayette, page 136
Nicole LeCour for UL Lafayette, page 139
Robin May, pages vi, viii
Janet Romero, page 125
Michael P. Smith © The Historic New Orleans Collection, acc. no. 2007.0103.4.704, page 25
Andy Snow, page 140

DESIGN

Dave Hussong
Megan Barra
Todd Ostendorf

SUPPORT

Dr. Walter B. Comeaux, Jr.
Walter 'Sonny' Comeaux, III
Clark Comeaux
Jim and Ginger Roy
Steve and Martha Abshire
Merilyn and George Crain
Frank and Peggy Camalo
Gene and Kathy Brierre
Dr. Scott Gremillion
Lucy Henke
Acadiana Center for the Arts
Joel Savoy, Louisiana Crossroads Series
Dr. Joshua Caffery and the staff of the Center for Louisiana Studies
University of Louisiana at Lafayette Press
University of Louisiana at Lafayette Foundation

To contribute to the scholarship fund for students enrolled in the Dr. Tommy Comeaux Traditional Music Program contact UL Lafayette Development gift@louisiana.edu or call 337 482-0922

Fender
Twin-Amp